THE GREEN BOOK OF SOUTH CAROLINA

The Green Book

of SOUTH CAROLINA

A GUIDE TO AFRICAN AMERICAN CULTURAL SITES

HUB CITY PRESS
SPARTANBURG, SC

Book Design Lead: Meg Reid

Hub City Editors: Betsy Teter, Kendall Owens, Brad Steinecke

Proofreaders: Rebecca Avakian, Susan Baker

Printed in the United States of America.

The Green Book of South Carolina is funded by grants from the City of Spartanburg and the Denny's Corporation.

SPECIAL SALES

This book is available at special discounts for bulk purchases. For more information, email orders@hubcity.org.

HUB CITY
PRESS

200 Ezell Street, Suite 1
Spartanburg, SC 29306
www.hubcity.org

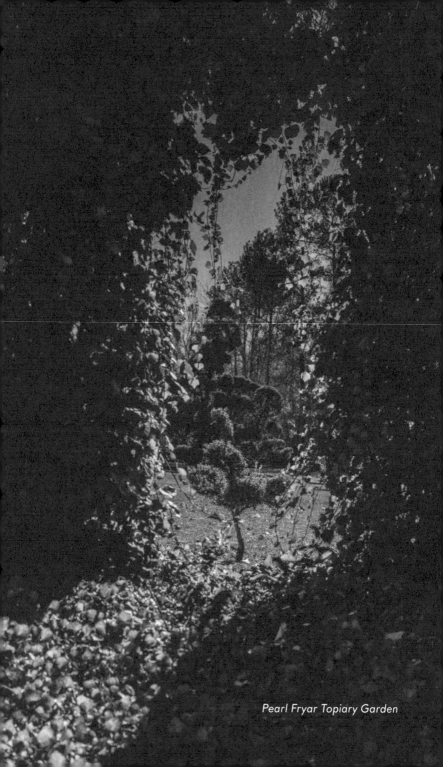

Pearl Fryar Topiary Garden

WELCOME TO THE GREEN BOOK OF SOUTH CAROLINA!

A Travel Guide to South Carolina African American Cultural Sites

The guidebook you hold in your hands is a print version of the Green Book of South Carolina, an award-winning online guide to more than 300 African American historic and cultural sites across the state. The online guide was created by the South Carolina African American Heritage Commission in 2017 and is a user-friendly platform that offers residents and visitors avenues to discover intriguing history and hidden gems about African Americans as they travel across the state. The most visitor-friendly places from the website are collected here in an accessible paperback edition.

Alongside these entries are photographs by Joshua Parks. Joshua traveled the state, meeting with descendants and community leaders at these sites. The resulting photographs are both artful and illuminating. They show us the beauty of South Carolina's landscape and the deep resilience of its people. As he puts it in his Photographer's Note (page xv), "It is my hope that *The Green Book of South Carolina* will illuminate the contributions of Africans and their descendants and will inspire others to continue their work, furthering Black people's collective struggle for freedom of movement, bodily autonomy, and self determination."

We hope you'll use this book for travel, vacations, and educational purposes. We know you'll discover how rich the Palmetto State is in incredible places that played a part in our nation's most significant moments.

TABLE OF CONTENTS

FOREWORD

DR. DARLENE CLARK HINE

THE year 2026 will mark 500 years since the first Africans arrived in what is today South Carolina. Spanish Viceroy Lucas Vasquez de Ayllon led an expedition of 500 people including enslaved Africans who settled along the coast, possibly on the Pee Dee River near present-day Georgetown. The settlement of San Miguel de Guadalupe did not last. It collapsed due to disease, disputes over leadership, conflicts with Native Americans, and insurrections by the enslaved Africans. The Africans rebelled and set fire to buildings, beginning what would become a long tradition of resistance in the Lowcountry. Some of the Africans escaped to the interior, beginning another long tradition among Black people. Although San Miguel de Guadalupe was abandoned after a few months, some of the Africans who had fled in all likelihood remained behind. Residing among Native Americans, they were here nearly 100 years before the first Africans arrived at Jamestown in 1619 and almost 150 years before the English and additional enslaved Africans settled Charles Town and the Carolina Colony in 1670.

No colony and no state has been more influenced by the presence of Africans and their descendants than South Carolina.

From the early 1700s until the 1920s—with the exception of a few years in the late 1700s and early 1800s—Black people constituted a majority of South Carolina's population. As many as 100,000 enslaved Africans who survived the horrors of the Middle Passage arrived at Gadsden's Wharf on the Cooper River in 18th-century Charleston. Today it is the location of the International African American Museum.

These enslaved people labored millions of hours on thousands of acres of rice fields in the Lowcountry. They did the difficult, dangerous, and often deadly work that made South Carolina the center of global rice production in the 18th century. That labor and that rice also made the planters some of the richest men in the English Empire. With the invention of the cotton gin came the rapid expansion of cotton planting in the 19th century, and the system of enslaved labor spread rapidly to the Carolina upcountry. By 1860 on the eve of the Civil War, South Carolina was home to 402,000 enslaved human beings, 58 percent of the state's population.

Any attempt to understand African American history begins in this state. When Stanley Harrold, William Hine, and I began more than 20 years ago to write the college history textbook that became *The African American Odyssey*, a New York editor at Prentice Hall wondered if we were not putting too much emphasis on South Carolina in providing a history of the African American experience. Our answer was an emphatic, "No!" The key to grasping that experience begins in South Carolina, and it continues to the present day.

It is impossible to go more than a few miles in any direction in South Carolina without encountering examples of the cultural, spiritual, and economic influence of Black Carolinians as well as examples of their resistance and resilience. Glance through this *Green Book*. Take a look at some of the important figures and meaningful places where people have lived, worked, prayed, played, and died. They contributed immeasurably to making this state and this nation what it is nearly 500 years after those first Africans arrived on these shores.

PENN CENTER ON STREET HELENA ISLAND. It was established by missionaries from the North as a school for freedmen in 1862 during the Civil War. Civil rights leaders, including Dr. Martin Luther King Jr., gathered here in 1963 to conduct planning sessions for the civil rights movement. Today it is part of the Reconstruction Era National Park.

STONO REBELLION. The largest slave rebellion in colonial America occurred in September 1739 near the Rantowles community on US Route 17 west of Charleston. At least 50 Black and white people died in the violent uprising as enslaved people attempted to escape to freedom in Spanish Florida.

ROBERT SMALLS. He earned enduring fame as the enslaved pilot of the Confederate ship, The Planter, when he and crew members seized the vessel and sailed it to the Union Naval blockade in May 1862. He fled with his wife, Hannah, their three children, and 13 other enslaved people. Smalls went on to a long political career in the State House and in the US House of Representatives.

ATLANTIC BEACH. This was one of the few places where Black people could enjoy themselves along the Atlantic coast during the Jim Crow era. Located north of Myrtle Beach, it featured hotels, nightclubs, and restaurants that were crowded with Black visitors from the 1930s to the 1960s.

STEPHEN SWAILS. His home was in Kingstree after he arrived during the Civil War with the famed 54th Massachusetts Regiment. He was one of the few Black officers to serve in the US Army during the war. He later became a prominent attorney and an influential state senator.

MARY MCLEOD BETHUNE. She was born in Mayesville in 1875. She was instrumental in founding Bethune-Cookman College (later University) in Daytona Beach, Florida. She also founded the National Conference of Negro Women in 1935. She was a member of President Franklin D. Roosevelt's "Black Cabinet" and a close confidant of his wife, Eleanor.

DR. MATILDA A. EVANS. She took up residence in Columbia after earning her medical degree, and she was one of the first women, Black or white, to practice medicine in South Carolina. She founded two hospitals for Black patients. She emphasized public health and provided free clinics that vaccinated hundreds of Black youngsters in the 1920s and 1930s.

MCCRORY'S FIVE AND DIME. Friendship Junior College students in Rock Hill participated in the first civil rights protests in South Carolina in 1960 and 1961 when they sat-in at the McCrory's lunch counter. In 1961 nine of those students refused to post bail after they were arrested during a sit-in. The "Friendship Nine" boasted "Jail, no bail!"

BENJAMIN E. MAYS. His birthplace near Epworth has been moved to become part of the Mays Museum in Greenwood. The legendary educator and theologian served as the president of Morehouse

College in Atlanta from 1940 to 1967. He was the mentor to many students including Martin Luther King Jr. Mays delivered the eulogy at King's funeral in 1968.

ORANGEBURG MASSACRE. On the night of February 8, 1968, on the campus of South Carolina State College (now University), South Carolina highway patrolmen opened fire on unarmed students demonstrating on the campus. Three students died and at least 28 were injured in the state's most tragic episode during the civil rights era.

MOTHER EMANUEL AME CHURCH. In 1865 Rev. Richard H. Cain established this church in Charleston. Cain became a prominent political leader during Reconstruction and served in the US House of Representatives. On June 17, 2015, a white supremacist shot and killed nine parishioners during Bible study. Rev. Clementa Pinckney was among those slain. He was also a state senator.

There are literally hundreds of other people and places in this *Green Book*. Take advantage of it. Use it. Increase your understanding of the crucial role played by African Americans in South Carolina.

PHOTOGRAPHER'S NOTE

THE fertile soil of South Carolina holds immaculate records of the African struggle for human dignity and freedom. Beyond Hollywood's pictorial plantations, the state's landscapes also offer up the marshy swamplands of the Lowcountry and its Sea Islands, the deep red clay of the Piedmont, and the rolling plateaus of the Sandhills. The bottom of man-made lakes and ponds, near where Black people once lived, and the remnants of the abandoned rice fields they once toiled, contain secrets of history that only those who found shade under South Carolina's haunting oak trees could tell. What we do know is that here Africans and their descendants lived, built communal structures, and fostered organizations that have had profound impacts on the state's social, political, and economic ways of life. I am a direct descendant of the captive Africans brought to South Carolina in bondage only a few generations ago, and this project has become a personal homage to both people and place. It is my hope that *The Green Book of South Carolina* will illuminate the contributions of Africans and their descendants and will inspire others to continue their work, furthering Black people's collective struggle for freedom of movement, bodily autonomy, and self determination.

JOSHUA PARKS, 2022

THE UPSTATE

Union County Jail

SUGGESTED DAY TRIP

9 A.M. RICHLAND CEMETERY
Sunflower Street, Greenville
Time at site: 20 minutes

10 A.M. JOSH WHITE MEMORIAL
Corner of Hammond Street and Falls Park Way, Greenville
Time at site: 20 minutes

11:00 P.M. GREENVILLE COUNTY COURTHOUSE
130 South Main Street, Greenville
Time at site: 30 minutes

Drive time to Spartanburg: 40 minutes

12:30 P.M. LUNCH
Charlene's Home Cooking
1163 East Blackstock Road, Spartanburg (864-764-1111)

1:30 P.M. WOOLWORTH'S AND KRESS SIT-INS
100 Block of Main Street, Spartanburg
Time at site: 20 min

2:30 P.M. SOUTHSIDE CULTURAL MONUMENT
Intersection of South Converse Street and Hudson Barksdale Boulevard, Spartanburg
Time at site: 30 minutes

WESTSIDE COMMUNITY CENTER

1100 West Franklin Street, Anderson

This former equalization school has been transformed into a popular community center by local historian and City Councilperson Beatrice Thompson. Westside Community Center is a non-profit, community-based organization whose members are committed to enhancing the lives of needy citizens in the Anderson community. Westside Community Center is home to a variety of agencies and services, including AnMed Westside Medical Health Clinic, Westside Department of Health and Environmental Control, Anderson City Police Department PACE, YMCA Programs, and various youth and community programming. *Open Mon. through Fri., 9 a.m. to 3:30 p.m.*

DUNTON CHAPEL

320 E. Buford Street, Gaffney

The first school for African American students in Gaffney was opened at this church in 1899 under the direction of Rev. R.C. Campbell. By 1920 it remained as one of only 10 schools in the county that served African American students. A night school serving adults also was operated at Dunton Chapel. The grade school remained in operation into the 1920s. The church can trace its origins back to 1870. Originally known as the Church of Gaffney, it was renamed Dunton Chapel in 1888 to honor Dr. Lewis M. Dunton, presiding elder of the Greenville District of the Methodist Episcopal Church.

ANTHONY CRAWFORD MARKER

Court Square, State Highway 202, Abbeville

Before the Civil War, South Carolina relied on a plantation economy, and enslaved Africans outnumbered white residents. Dehumanized, brutalized, and treated as property, Black people resisted in ways small and large to survive. After the Confederacy's defeat, the 13th, 14th, and 15th Amendments to the US Constitution ended slavery and guaranteed Black citizenship rights. Reconstruction promised federal enforcement and gave African Americans hope for the future. Black men used their new voting rights and, in South Carolina, elected African American candidates to all levels of government. African Americans' political and economic advancement soon sparked resentment and violence. When federal protection ended in 1877, lynching—or murder at the hands of a mob—became a tool for re-establishing white supremacy and terrorizing the Black community. White mobs lynched more than 4,000 Black people in the South between 1877 and 1950, and more than 180 of them were killed in South Carolina. In addition to Anthony Crawford in 1916, at least seven other men were lynched in Abbeville County during the era: Dave Roberts (1882); James Mason (1894); Thomas Watts and John Richards (1895); Allen Pendleton (1905); Will Lozier (1915); and Mark Smith (1919).

In Abbeville on Saturday, October 21, 1916, a white mob lynched a Black leader named Anthony Crawford for cursing a white man. A 56-year-old planter, "Grandpa" Crawford owned 427 acres of land, had 13 children, and helped establish a school, a church, and farms in the local Black community. During the Jim Crow era, successful Black people were conspicuous—and

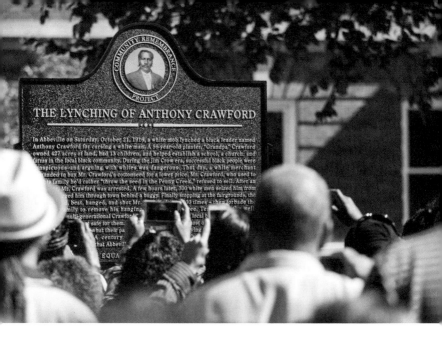

THE LYNCHING OF ANTHONY CRAWFORD

In Abbeville on Saturday, October 21, 1916, a white mob lynched a black leader named Anthony Crawford for cursing a white man. A 56-year-old planter, "Grandpa" Crawford owned 427 acres of land, had 13 children, and helped establish a school, a church, and farms in the local black community. During the Jim Crow era, successful black people were conspicuous—and arguing with whites was dangerous. That day, a white merchant demanded to buy Mr. Crawford's cottonseed for a lower price. Mr. Crawford, who used to tell his family he'd rather "throw the seed in the Penny Creek," refused to sell. After an argument, Mr. Crawford was arrested. A few hours later, 300 white men seized him from jail and dragged him through town behind a buggy. Finally stopping at the fairgrounds, the mob stabbed, beat, hanged, and shot Mr. Crawford over 200 times — then forbade the family to remove his hanging body from the tree. ... multi-generational Crawford ... safe for them. ... that their pa ... A century ... that Abbevil' EQUA

arguing with whites was dangerous. That day, a white merchant demanded to buy Mr. Crawford's cottonseed for a lower price. Mr. Crawford, who used to tell his family he'd rather "throw the seed in the Penny Creek," refused to sell. After an argument, Mr. Crawford was arrested. A few hours later, 300 white men seized him from jail and dragged him through town behind a buggy. Finally stopping at the fairgrounds, the mob stabbed, beat, hanged and shot Mr. Crawford over 200 times—then forbade the Crawford family to remove his hanging body from the tree. Terrorized, the well-established, multi-generational Crawford family and many other local Black people realized that Abbeville was not safe for them. Amid continued threats, most of the family scattered North, leaving behind what their patriarch had built, and carrying the painful loss of his wisdom and humor. A century later, this marker symbolizes their continued remembrance—and hope that Abbeville would never forget or repeat that horrendous October day.

BENJAMIN E. MAYS BIRTHPLACE

237 N. Hospital Street, Greenwood

This house is the birthplace of Dr. Benjamin E. Mays (1894-1984), Baptist minister, college president, author, and civil rights pioneer. It was originally located 14 miles from this site in the Epworth community. Mays was the eighth child of Hezekiah and Louvenia Mays, both born into slavery. He was a graduate of Bates College and the University of Chicago and was an early and forceful opponent of segregation. Mays served as Dr. Martin Luther King's "spiritual mentor" during his tenure as president of Morehouse College in Atlanta (1940-1967). His inspiring memoir *Born To Rebel: An Autobiography* (1971) is a classic civil rights text. Mays' childhood home was moved to its current location, renovated, and dedicated as a museum in 2011.

RICHLAND CEMETERY

Sunflower Street, Greenville

In 1884 the city of Greenville established this cemetery on the banks of Richland Creek. Today these six acres serve as the final resting place for more than 1,400 African Americans, including some of the most influential Black citizens of Greenville. Located on a hill overlooking Stone Avenue, it also is on the US National Register of Historic Places. Among those buried here are William Sewell, Greenville's first African American licensed contractor; Hattie Logan Duckett, founder of the Phillis Wheatley Center; writer/activist Elias Holloway, Greenville's first Black letter carrier; and Cora Kilgore Chapman, Greenville's first Black nurse.

SPRINGFIELD BAPTIST CHURCH

600 E. McBee Avenue, Greenville

Organized in 1867 by 65 freedmen and led by Rev. Gabriel Poole, Springfield Baptist later became the headquarters of the non-violent civil rights movement in Greenville in the 1960s. On Jan. 1, 1960, the church organized a 1,000-person march to the Greenville Downtown Airport after baseball star Jackie Robinson was denied use of the airport's waiting room when he arrived to address the state convention of the NAACP. Robinson, the first African American to play Major League baseball, was in attendance at the march.

Numerous sit-ins at Greenville lunch counters also were organized at Springfield Baptist. In 1963 church member A.J. Wittenburg filed the lawsuit that led to the integration of Greenville County schools. The original church burned in 1972 and was replaced with the present building, though the church's first bell remains a part of the new marquee. Springfield Baptist Church is the only Upstate site on the US Civil Rights Trail.

HISTORIC RICHLAND CEMETERY

MONUMENT TO JOSH WHITE

Corner of Hammond Street and Falls Park Way, Greenville

Born Feb. 11, 1914, Joshua Daniel "Josh" White performed on the streets of his Greenville hometown before moving to New York City in 1930 to become a prolific and much-recorded bluesman. White recorded the first million-selling single by a Black performer, "One Meatball." He also performed for President Franklin Roosevelt, starred on Broadway, and released two racially charged protest albums.

A bronze relief sculpture by Joe Thompson honoring the boundary-breaking Black musician was unveiled in downtown Greenville in 2021. The sculpture includes words from White's testimony before the US House Committee on Un-American Activities when he had to testify in his own defense.

THE WILLIE EARLE LYNCHING TRIAL

130 South Main Street, Greenville

The largest lynching trial in U.S. history was held here May 12-21, 1947. Willie Earle, a young black man accused of assaulting white cabdriver Thomas W. Brown, had been lynched by a white mob on Bramlett Road in Greenville. The trial of 31 whites, 28 of them cabdrivers, was rare at the time and drew national attention. Though 26 defendants admitted being part of the mob, all defendants were acquitted by an all-white jury. Rebecca West's "Opera in Greenville," published in *The New Yorker* on June 14, 1947, interpreted the trial and its aftermath. Widespread outrage over the lynching and the verdict spurred new federal civil rights policies.

171 RIVER PLACE

Monument to Josh White

CLAUSSEN BAKERY

400 Augusta Street, Greenville

In February 1967, 22 African American employees went on strike to protest discrimination in hiring and promotion practices at the local bakery. The Greenville branch of the NAACP called for a boycott of Claussen baked goods in protest. Jesse Jackson, then working as director of SCLC's Operation Breadbasket, helped bring Rev. Martin Luther King Jr. to Greenville on April 30, 1967. King, who spoke to 3,500 people at the Greenville Memorial Auditorium, preached economic justice and support for the Claussen workers who "had been called boys...then they stood up like men."

STERLING HIGH SCHOOL MARKER

Corner of Calhoun and Pendleton streets, Greenville

Sterling was the first Black public high school in Greenville County. It originated from an 1896 school opened by Rev. D.M. Minus called Greenville Academy. In 1902 it moved from West Greenville and was then renamed Sterling Industrial College after Mrs. E.R. Sterling, who had financed Rev. Minus's education at Claflin University. In 1929 it was bought by the county school district and renamed Sterling High School. On Sept. 15, 1967, a fire began at a high school dance and the school burned to the ground. The marker on site was erected in 2007 by the Greenville County Historical Commission and the Sterling High School Association.

THE BIRTHPLACE OF JESSE JACKSON

20 Haynie Street, Greenville

Though not open for tours, the modest house at 20 Haynie Street in Greenville is the birthplace of Jesse Jackson, founder of the Rainbow PUSH Coalition, a two-time presidential candidate, and recipient of the U.S. Medal of Freedom. His mother, Helen Burns Jackson, was 16 when she gave birth to the future civil rights icon on Oct. 8, 1941 in the three-room house. As a teenager, Jackson and seven others staged a sit-in at the whites-only Greenville County Public Library on July 15, 1960. Known as the "Greenville Eight," all of them were National Honor Society members and each was forcibly removed and spent part of the day in jail. The library closed for two weeks but reopened as an integrated facility.

THE GREENVILLE COUNTY MUSEUM OF ART

420 College Street, Greenville

This museum has one of the world's most extensive collections of artwork created by African American artists from South Carolina, including the largest institutional collection of clay vessels made by enslaved Edgefield artisan David "Dave the Potter" Drake. The museum houses the largest collection of paintings outside of the Smithsonian by William H. Johnson, an African American artist and Florence native who achieved great success in Europe.

More than 50 works are included in this exhibition that explores the viewpoint of African-American artists. The earliest examples are clay vessels made by enslaved potter and poet David Drake along with an 1850 painting View of Asheville, North Carolina by free man of color Robert Duncanson.

The exhibition also features works by such 20th-century luminaries as William H. Johnson, Romare Bearden, and Jacob Lawrence. More contemporary highlights include Kara Walker, Carrie Mae Weems, Leo Twiggs, Gary Grier, and Jonathan Green.

Alongside *Masterworks of Color*, the GCMA also presents *In a Mirror, Darkly*, which examines the issues and images created when white artists portray black subjects and experiences, and Carew Rice, a retrospective of the renowned Lowcountry silhouettist's works from the 1930s through the 1960s. *Open Wed. through Sat., 10 a.m. to 5 p.m.; Sun. 1-5 p.m.*

BELL STREET SCHOOL / MARTHA DENDY SCHOOL

301 N. Bell Street, Clinton

Built in 1926, Bell Street School was the second school built on this site for African Americans. The first was Friendship School, founded in 1883 by the Friendship AME Church. Roughly a decade later, Bell Street School became the first Black high school in Laurens County to earn its accreditation. It was converted into an elementary school when the county built a new high school. The school was renamed Martha Dendy Elementary, in honor of the mother of principal David Dendy, in 1960. The school closed in 2008.

HOPEWELL ROSENWALD SCHOOL

253 Hopewell Church Road, Clarks Hill

Built in 1926, Hopewell is the only Rosenwald School remaining in McCormick County. Hopewell greatly impacted the education of rural McCormick County's African American students from 1927 to 1954. By 1954 Hopewell's enrollment dropped to only nine students as many of the African American families left the area for better opportunities. The school was then left for the benefit and use of the community. African American schools, especially in rural counties such as McCormick, were extremely important in the education they provided, the safe environment they gave, and the belief that if students studied and did their best, they could improve their lives.

BERTHA LEE STRICKLAND CULTURAL MUSEUM

208 W. South 2nd Street, Seneca

Bertha Lee Strickland Cultural Museum is the only exhibit museum in Oconee County that underscores the rich, colorful, turbulent history of the local African American community. As stated in its motto, "Honoring the Past— Elevating the Future," the museum incorporates technology and tradition to create a meaningful and educational experience for all ages. Rotating exhibits two to four times annually, BLSCM showcases ordinary people of the past and present whose stories and achievements will impact generations.

Open Weds. through Sat., 11 a.m. to 4 p.m.
Admission is free.

Pictured below: Ms. Shelby Henderson, Director of the Bertha Lee Strickland Cultural Museum

The Bertha Lee Strickland Cultural Museum is unique in the Upcountry, where African American history is not often preserved.

AFRICAN AMERICA
CEMETERY SITE

BURIALS OF
ENSLAVED PEOPLE,
SHARECROPPERS,
DOMESTIC LABORER
AND
CONVICTED LABORER

FORT HILL SLAVE QUARTERS / CLEMSON COLLEGE CONVICT STOCKADE

Fernow Street, Clemson

Located one-eighth mile from the main plantation house, the Fort Hill slave quarters were described in 1849 as being "built of stone and joined together like barracks, with gardens attached." Some 70-80 enslaved African Americans then lived at Fort Hill. In 1854 Andrew P. Calhoun moved to Fort Hill from Alabama with his slaves. At his death in 1865, the estate included 139 enslaved African Americans. In 1890 convicted laborers, mostly African Americans, were jailed in a prison stockade nearby. They cleared land and made and laid bricks. They also dismantled the stone slave quarters to use as foundations for Clemson College's earliest buildings.

In 2013, while conducting a historical survey of African American life in Pickens, Oconee, and Anderson counties, Dr. Rhondda Thomas found the names and records of the convict laborers—nearly 700 men and boys—who built Clemson University's first buildings. She realized that their names must be remembered, and began Call My Name to document all aspects of African American history in the Clemson area.

Pictured at left: Dr. Rhondda Thomas, Calhoun Lemon Professor of Literature, Clemson University

HARVEY GANTT MARKER

Near Tillman Hall, Clemson

Clemson University became the first white college or university in the state to integrate after Reconstruction. Harvey B. Gantt, a Charleston native wanting to study architecture, applied for admission in 1961. When Clemson delayed admitting him, he sued in federal court in the summer of 1962. President Robert C. Edwards, meanwhile, worked behind the scenes to make plans for Gantt's eventual enrollment. Edwards and several leading businessmen, politicians, and others drew up an elaborate plan, described as "a conspiracy for peace," designed to ensure that Gantt would enter Clemson without the protests and violence that marked the integration of other Southern universities. After a federal court ruled that Clemson should admit him, Gantt enrolled without incident. He graduated with honors in 1965.

SOAPSTONE BAPTIST CHURCH

26 Liberia Road, Pickens

Soapstone Baptist Church is the anchor of the Liberia community, a Black freedom colony, located in Pickens County. Established after the Civil War, the church built a school to educate area children. Jim Crow threatened the community's vitality as Black landowners in Liberia lost their land and racial violence sped migration. African Americans in Liberia resisted, survived, and thrived despite this culture of terror and the persistent inequalities caused by segregation.

In April 1967, arsonists burned the old sanctuary. White neighbors and Black residents contributed their time, labor, money, and love to rebuild the church and fellowship hall.

OLD CITY CEMETERY

Cemetery Street, Spartanburg

This public graveyard includes the remains of many slaves and early freedmen who were originally buried in Spartanburg's first African American village cemetery, which was located west of Morgan Square near the railroad crossing. When the railyards there were expanded around 1910, those bodies were exhumed and moved to this site. Prominent persons buried here include: educator Mary Honor Farrow Wright, for whom Mary Wright School was named; midwife Phyllis Goins; policeman Tobe Hartwell; City Councilman Thomas Bomar; and educator Addie Wright McWhirter, first woman to teach at the South Carolina School for the Deaf and Blind. It remains in use to the present day.

MOUNT MORIAH BAPTIST CHURCH

445 South Church Street, Spartanburg

Mount Moriah Baptist Church began in a brush arbor soon after Emancipation. A founding father of the church was Joseph Young, who had often preached to the Black members of Spartanburg's First Baptist Church before the Civil War. In 1870 he donated land on South Liberty Street, which by 1877 included a brick church, said to be the first built by a Black congregation in South Carolina. The church's first pastors were Rev. Julius Steel and Rev. W. Murray Evans. Later pastors included Rev. Joel L. King, an uncle of Dr. Martin Luther King Jr. The Lincoln School, the first graded public school for Black children in Spartanburg, opened in the basement of Mount Moriah in 1884, and in later years, the church hosted graduation exercises for many local schools. The cornerstone and bell of the 1912 church remain in the courtyard behind the chapel of the current sanctuary, built in 1976.

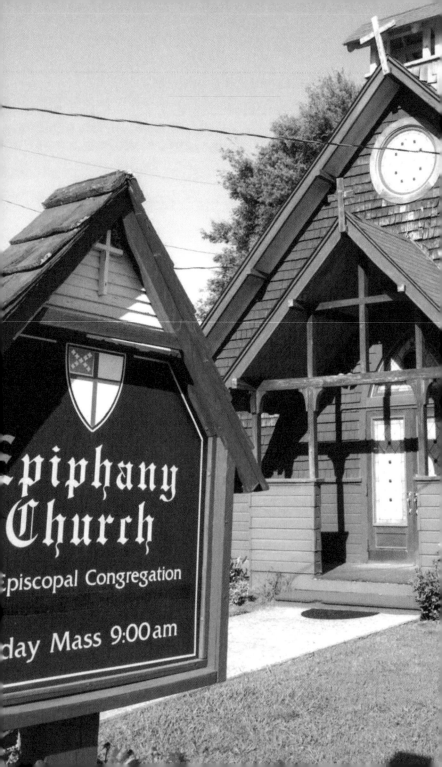

THE EPISCOPAL CHURCH OF THE EPIPHANY

410 S. Liberty Street, Spartanburg

The Episcopal Church of the Epiphany, built in 1912, was where the Black Episcopalians of this area went to worship. It is the oldest surviving African American church building in the city and is the only physical structure remaining from the old South Liberty Street community, most of which was torn down in Urban Renewal in the 1970s.

Though this structure was built in 1912, the congregation first met independently of the predominantly-white Episcopal Church of the Advent in 1893. Widely known for its kindergarten, this church also hosted numerous community meetings related to the struggle for equal rights during the 1950s and 1960s.

MARY H. WRIGHT ELEMENTARY SCHOOL

201 Caulder Avenue, Spartanburg

Mary H. Wright Elementary is the first site to commemorate educator Mary Honor Farrow Wright, whose high morals and lengthy activism in many areas did much to open opportunities for African Americans in Spartanburg during the early 20th century. It opened in the 1951-52 school year, and Charlie B. Hauser served as its first principal. After serving as a school for 50 years, the building housed public offices, and in 2022 is undergoing a renovation to become the Schoolhouse Lofts development.

WOODWARD FUNERAL HOME

594 Howard Street, Spartanburg

Established in 1916, J. W. Woodward Funeral Home is the oldest Black-owned business in Spartanburg and is located in a building that once served as the home of Thomas M. Bomar, Spartanburg's first African American City Council member. After Bomar's death in 1904, his widow, Carrie Bomar Perry, would operate various businesses from her home, including the Provident Hospital, a private hospital for African Americans that operated for much of the 1920s. This building has served as the Woodward Funeral Home since 1946.

Pictured below: The Woodward Family (Left to right: James "Tee" Ferguson Jr. Dr. Kay Woodward, and Stinson Ferguson)

GAS BOTTOM

E. Daniel Morgan Avenue and N. Pine Street, Spartanburg

For its size, Spartanburg received a significant amount of federal funding for Urban Renewal efforts between the 1950s and 1970s. The first area in the city to receive attention, with a mixture of rehabilitation and demolition, was the former neighborhood known as Gas Bottom, so-called because of the natural gas electrical plant in the same valley. This had been one of the poorest African American areas of the city, plagued by pollution and poor sanitation controls. The mid-1950s extension of a major highway, North Pine Street, and a mixture of local and federal Urban Renewal funding dramatically changed the area. This was the first federally-funded Urban Renewal project area in South Carolina.

ALEXANDER ELEMENTARY/DEAN STREET SCHOOL

312 North Dean Street, Spartanburg

In 1891 Spartanburg Black public schools were consolidated into the Dean Street School, which served students in grades 1-7 until 1915 when it added eighth and ninth graders. After a fire and extensive renovation, it was renamed Alexander Elementary School in 1939 in honor of R.M. Alexander, who served as principal for 30 years. Alexander closed in 1970 after educating Black students in Spartanburg for 71 years. Today the building serves as the local headquarters of Omega Psi Phi.

SOUTH LIBERTY STREET

Spartanburg

The Southside Black community was established soon after Emancipation by families who fled the racial and political tensions of white-dominant spaces in downtown Spartanburg and established a new community along South Liberty Street. This area functioned like a separate downtown, with business and residential districts, and families of varying wealth and influence. Among the most influencial people to own land and lead the neighborhood were Joseph and Priscilla Young. The Youngs donated property on South Liberty Street for the purpose of building Mount Moriah Baptist Church. In 1884 the Spartanburg Board of Education selected the basement of Mount Moriah Baptist Church as the location for the first school for Spartanburg's "colored community" and named it the Lincoln School. In later years, this neighborhood included other public schools such as Carrier Street School and Carver High School. During World War II, South Liberty Street included a USO, where Black soldiers came for recreation. Black teachers and doctors built their homes on South Liberty Street, and businesses were also abundant during the early and middle 20th century. By 1970, the Southside community had grown in population and was well-established with Black businesses and families. When the

Pictured at right: Former South Carolina Representative Brenda Lee Pryce and former Spartanburg Mayor James E. Talley

federally-funded program known as Urban Renewal came to the Southside community, it destroyed the hopes and dreams of the families living there, with promises of a rejuvenated landscape remaining unmaterialized even decades later. Spartanburg City razed 40 city blocks where over 2,000 people lived. Local activist James Cheek called it "an American tragedy."

GEORGE WASHINGTON
CARVER
HIGH SCHOOL

Carver High School first opened its doors to Spartanburg students in 1939. At that time the stately red-brick building became the only African-American High School in the city and originally housed twelve classrooms. Throughout its 63-year history, numerous expansions occurred, and in 1970 the school became a proud high school when the two district high schools were merged. In 2002 the original building was replaced with a new facility, and the tradition of providing quality education on the South Church Street campus continued.

DR. T. K. GREGG HOME

237 North Dean Street, Spartanburg

Born in 1902, Dr. Theodore K. Gregg was the fifth child of Rev. Lexington and Eliza Gregg. Rev. Gregg moved his family to Spartanburg to become the pastor at Silver Hill Methodist Church. Theodore attended Maharry Medical College in Nashville, TN and interned at St. Agnes Hospital in Raleigh, NC. Dr. Gregg returned to Spartanburg in 1930, opened his medical practice on North Church Street and bought a house on North Dean Street, near Silver Hill AME and his family's residence at Silver Hill's parsonage on North Converse Street.

Dr. Gregg was an active member of the community and led the effort to establish a much-needed community and recreation center for Black youth. He organized multiple fundraising activities, including a "Negro Spiritual Program" concert held at the Carolina Theater in 1936, and worked with the National Youth Association, the WPA, and local groups to raise funds. Dr. Gregg died suddenly in 1939 before the recreation center was built. The T.K. Gregg Recreation Center located at 650 Howard Street was named in his honor for his commitment to improving Black life in Spartanburg.

CALLAHAM FUNERAL HOME

228 North Dean Street, Spartanburg

Founded by Nina and Worth Littlejohn in 1913, the John-Nina Hospital was the first and only licensed Black hospital in Spartanburg. The Littlejohns, who lived next door to the hospital, were active members of the community and determined to establish a hospital for Black people in town. The hospital provided comfortable surroundings for up to 36 patients who were fed from a vegetable garden that sat behind the building. The John-Nina Hospital was merged with Spartanburg Hospital in 1932, and R.W. Callaham, a successful businessman and funeral director from Anderson, purchased the building in 1933. Callaham Funeral Home stood for 74 years until a fire destroyed it in 2007. The new building was completed in 2010.

FAIRFOREST PARK

500 Highland Avenue, Spartanburg

Fairforest Park, now known as Edward C. Stewart Park, was the first city park for African Americans in Spartanburg, created in 1949 through a donation by the Spartanburg County Foundation. Originally it was 18 acres in size and by the early 1950s also included playground equipment, a picnic area, a swimming pool, a wading pool, and a bath house. The park now includes basketball courts, a splashpad playground, a covered pavilion, trails, and a multi-purpose field.

BACK OF THE COLLEGE MEMORIAL

551 Cumming Street, Spartanburg

The Back of the College neighborhood memorial was erected on the Wofford College campus in February 1998 at a ceremony that included Hattie Bell Penland, a 95-year-old former resident and much admired teacher. Members of the Wofford Neighborhood Focus Group, a collaboration between college students and local Black leaders designed to establish better relations between college and community, and Winston Wingo, the artist who sculpted the memorial, braved cold temperatures to install the memorial.

The Back of the College—called so by many of its residents—was the oldest predominantly Black neighborhood in Spartanburg. Founded in 1869 with the consecration of Silver Hill Methodist

Church, the neighborhood grew rapidly to encompass more than 300 houses at its peak in the 1940s, the city's first stand-alone primary and secondary public schools for Black students, five churches, and generations of families whose stories helped to make Spartanburg what it is today.

CUMMING STREET SCHOOL

640 Cumming Street, Spartanburg

The first public junior high and high school to serve Black students in Spartanburg, the Cumming Street School opened in 1926 after pressure from local community members who argued that Black students deserved the opportunity to pursue secondary education. It opened to students in grades 1-9 and then briefly added tenth and eleventh grades before Carver High School opened in 1938. Principal E.B. Coleman led Cumming Street with a firm and steady hand until Spartanburg public schools desegregated in 1970. The school remained open for individual and specialized instruction until the building was condemned for asbestos contamination in 1982. Cumming Street School helped to anchor the Back of the College community. Teachers and students lived in the neighborhood, attended its proms, pageants, and festivals, competed in its athletic events, and held community gatherings on its grounds. Wofford College purchased the building from Spartanburg's District 7 schools in 2008.

Pictured above: Former Cumming Street School student Nannie Jefferies

WOOLWORTH'S AND KRESS SIT-INS

100 Block of East Main Street, Spartanburg

In the spring and summer of 1960, African Americans across the South began challenging whites-only lunch counters by taking a seat anyway, knowing that the business would refuse to serve them. The sit-ins sparked a backlash, and on July 25, 1960, Spartanburg City Council passed a law making it a misdemeanor to refuse to leave an establishment immediately when so requested by the proprietor or manager. Until that point, Spartanburg had been without any sit-in demonstrations. The next day, a group of nine Carver High School students sat at the Woolworth's lunch counter and remained sitting until the lunch counter was closed. The manager followed company policy and did not serve them nor ask them to leave. Police officers and a large crowd gathered to watch the demonstration, but no violence was reported. Larger crowds gathered the next day as 25 demonstrators sat for one hour at the Kress lunch counter. The event turned hostile when two white men struck two demonstrators in the neck and chest. The demonstrators raised their arms but did not hit back. Police apprehended all four of them. The crowds disbursed and the newspaper reported that throughout the afternoon, larger groups of whites could be seen trailing behind smaller Black groups throughout the entire downtown area. Shouts and curses were exchanged in several cases and "police were dispatched to various tense spots during the day." By nightfall, there had been five arrests, and a statement had been issued by City Council warning demonstrators and

WOOLWORTH'S SIT IN

On July 26, 1960, a group of black youths sat at the lunch counter in Woolworth's, a chain department store once located at this site, as a demonstration against the store's all-white policy for lunch counter service. The demonstration occurred the day after Spartanburg City Council passed a proclamation against sit-ins. The sit-in at the Spartanburg Woolworth's initiated a series of civil rights protests in Spartanburg throughout the week including further sit-ins at Woolworth's and Kress's lunch counters.

Project of the Leadership Spartanburg Class of 2015

spectators that mass arrests would occur if crowds gathered on the following day. With the exception of a small, peaceful sit-in later in August, there were no more recorded lunch counter sit-ins. In June 1963 a voluntary committee of restaurant proprietors in the city announced that they would begin serving all races effective immediately.

HISTORIC DUNCAN PARK

1000 Duncan Park Drive, Spartanburg

Duncan Park was designed by Spartanburg architect J. Frank Collins in 1926 and one of the oldest baseball stadiums in the nation. It Before the integration of sports, Spartanburg had separate baseball teams, which each used the city's premier minor league baseball stadium at Duncan Park. Much of this stadium remains intact, including the separate bleacher section that was originally reserved for African Americans. Spartanburg's Negro League team were the Spartanburg Sluggers, which first organized in 1905 and remained active into the early 1950s. Beginning in 1921, the team was owned by early Black entrepreneur Newt Whitmire and his son, whose downtown restaurant also hosted many of the early greats of jazz. The Sluggers played other Negro League teams across the country and hosted many barnstorming teams that featured star players, including Bob Branson, Jackie Robinson, and Hank Aaron.

Pictured below: Mr. Luther Norman

EMANCIPATION JUBILEE FLAG

Spartanburg County Public Library HQ, Spartanburg

On September 22, 1865, Spartanburg's newly-freed African Americans celebrated their emancipation and honored the soldiers who had made it possible at a spring about one mile from the courthouse village. While defeated Confederates watched, Black organizers marched in a parade alongside Federal soldiers from the public square to this spring, where a luncheon was served to the soldiers. They carried with them a hand-sewn American flag that was presented to commanding officer Captain Norris Crossman by a Baptist preacher and his wife, tentatively identified as Joseph and Priscilla Young, who would soon after found the South Liberty Street neighborhood. The flag was rediscovered in 2015 and is now held by the public library at 151 South Church Street, in downtown Spartanburg.

BETHLEHEM CENTER

397 Highland Avenue, Spartanburg

This community center opened in 1930 as a mission activity by Bethel Methodist Church to provide daycare for African American children who were being left home alone while their mothers went to work. It originally operated out of a small house, but since 1950, it has been in its current facility, which was designed by Harold Woodward, a modernist Spartanburg architect known also for his design of the Spartanburg Downtown Airport building and other local modernist landmarks. The Bethlehem Center currently offers services for people of all ages and backgrounds.

HARLEM HELLFIGHTERS

W. O. Ezell and Westgate Mall Drive, Spartanburg

This roadside historic plaque commemorates the experience of the 15th New York National Guard, which briefly received training at Camp Wadsworth west of Spartanburg during World War I. These African American New Yorkers received harsh treatment from many local whites who expected them to submit to Jim Crow era social standards. As incidents of harassment and violence mounted, Army leadership agreed to cut their training short and send them to France, where they were the first American unit in combat. Widely commemorated for their bravery in battle, they received the nickname "the Harlem Hellfighters." They served at the front for 191 days, the longest of any American unit in World War I.

LITTLE AFRICA

Little Africa Road, and SC Highway 9, Chesnee

Little Africa was one of a number of independent African American communities formed across the South after the Civil War. Founded around 1880 by former slaves Simpson Foster and Emanuel Waddell, it was originally just a few acres set aside for their relatives. It grew to several hundred residents as other families settled nearby seeking economic opportunity and refuge from white supremacy. Many residents were farmers, and agriculture remained central to life in Little Africa for decades. By 1910 community leaders had built the two-room Africa School to teach local children. One of South Carolina's first Rosenwald Fund schools later opened there.

SIMS HIGH SCHOOL #2

200 Sims Drive, Union

Sims High School, located here from 1956 to 1970, replaced a 1927 school on Union Boulevard, which in 1929 had become the first state-accredited high school for African American students in the Upstate. It was named for Rev. A.A. Sims, founder and first principal (1927-1951). A new school was built here in 1956. Notable alumni include the first Black head coach in NCAA Division I-A football, the first coach of a Black college basketball team in the National Invitational Tournament, and the first Black chief of chaplains of the United States Army. Sims High School closed in 1970 with the desegregation of Union County schools, but this building housed Sims Junior High School from 1970 to 2009. A new Sims Middle School, on Whitmire Highway, opened in 2009.

CORINTH BAPTIST CHURCH

302 N. Herdon Street, Union

The first Black congregation in Union was organized in 1883 and first held services in the Old Union Methodist Church. The congregation purchased this lot in 1894 and constructed this late Gothic Revival-style building, which was added to the National Register of Historic Places in 1989.

The Union Remembrance Project, started in 2019, aims "to record, remember, and recognize the violent history of lynching and racial terrorism in Union County in order to foster justice and healing." The project is being conducted in partnership with the Equal Justice Initiative, a Montgomery, Alabama-based nonprofit working to end mass incarceration, excessive punishment, and racial inequality.

JAIL RAID OF 1871 MARKER

225 SC Highway 49, Union

On January 4 and February 12, 1871, white mobs abducted 12 Black men from the county jail. Captain J. Alexander Walker, Charner Gordon, Andrew Thompson, Sylvanus Wright, Barret Edwards, Thomas Byers, Aaron Thompson, Joseph Vanlue, Ellison Scott, William Fincher, Mac Bobo, and Amos McKissick were hanged or shot at the "hanging grounds" before any determination was made of their guilt. Ten of the 12 Black men were South Carolina state militia members who were accused of killing a white man named Mat Stevens while he was illegally transporting bootleg whiskey.

Months later, the U.S. Congress held hearings in former Confederate states to investigate incidents of racial violence, including the Union Jail Raid Massacre. No one was held accountable for this massacre.

In 2021 a marker was placed where the men were held in jail in what is today the offices of the Union County Sheriff's Office on West Main Street.

Pictured below: Timika Wilson, Union County Community Remembrance Project leader

McCrory's Five and Dime

THE MIDLANDS

Historic Brattonsville

SUGGESTED DAY TRIP

9 A.M. **AFRICAN AMERICAN MONUMENT ON STATE HOUSE GROUNDS**
Main and Gervais streets
Time at site: 45 minutes

10 A.M. **WALKING MAIN STREET TOUR**
Guided by ColumbiaSC63.com. Call 803-851-5064 or email
columbiasc63osm@gmail.com
**The State House and Main Street were settings for demonstrations and
protests, including sit-ins and marches. This tour helps explain some of
those defining moments in the civil rights movement.**
Time for tour: one hour

11:30 P.M. **LUNCH**
Cafeteria-style lunches served at United House of Prayer,
2426 Read Street, Columbia (803-748-0555)

1 P.M. **MANN-SIMONS SITE**
1403 Richland Street, Columbia (803-252-7742)
Time at site: one hour

2:15 P.M. **MODJESKA SIMKINS HOUSE**
2025 Marion Street, Columbia (803-252-7742)
Time at site: 30 minutes

3:15 P.M. **ALLEN UNIVERSITY HISTORIC DISTRICT**, incl. Chappelle Auditorium
1530 Harden Street, Columbia (803-376-5700)
Time at site: 30 minutes

REDCLIFFE PLANTATION STATE HISTORIC SITE

181 Redcliffe Road, Beech Island

Redcliffe interprets the history of multiple generations of families (Henleys, Goodwins, and Wigfalls) who were enslaved here and at other plantations owned by SC Governor James Henry Hammond, or who worked as sharecroppers and/or paid employees from 1831 to 1875. In addition to touring the two historic circa 1857 slave cabins, visitors can learn more from special exhibits and interpretive programs. The slave quarters, mansion, and iconic lane of 145-year old magnolia trees illustrate the plantation's history. The site includes a gift shop and hiking trail. *Open every day, 9 a.m. to 6 p.m.*

Other places that offer interpretive programming on African American heritage in state parks are Aiken State Park , Charles Towne Landing, Hampton Plantation, Lake Greenwood State Park and Rose Hill Plantation State Historic Site.

CENTER FOR AFRICAN AMERICAN HISTORY, ART AND CULTURE

120 York Street NE, Aiken

The Center for African American History, Art and Culture is housed in the historic Immanuel Institute. Rev. W.R. Coles, an African American Presbyterian missionary, moved to Aiken in 1881 and established a church and school for freed enslaved people. The Institute began in a six-room house on Newberry Street. As the student population grew, Coles built the Immanuel Institute in 1889. Over the years, the building has housed a variety of educational and cultural schools. Among them were Coles Academy, Coles Normal and Industrial School, Immanuel Institute, Jackson School, Andrew Roberts Institute, and St. Gerard Catholic School. The Immanuel Institute is listed on the National Register of Historic Places. CAAHAC is delighted to host lecture series, art shows, traveling exhibits, special events, concert series, and more. *Open Fri., 10 a.m. to 1 p.m. Tours by appointment only. Email info@caahac.org to set up an appointment.*

HAPPY HOME BAPTIST CHURCH

336 Railroad Avenue, Allendale

This church, founded soon after the Civil War, held its first services in a brush arbor in the Woods community of what was then Barnwell County. It built its first permanent church, a frame building, in the Zion Branch community near Old Allendale, and adopted the name Zion Branch Baptist Church. The church bought this site in 1875, built a new frame sanctuary here, and was renamed Happy Home Baptist Church.

VOORHEES COLLEGE

481 Porter Drive, Denmark

Voorhees College, founded by Elizabeth Evelyn Wright in 1897 as the Denmark Industrial School, was an effort to emphasize a vocational curriculum for rural African American students on the model of the Tuskegee Institute. The school, with funding from philanthropist Ralph Voorhees, was renamed Voorhees Industrial School for Colored Youth in 1904, Voorhees Normal and Industrial School in 1916, and Voorhees School and Junior College in 1947. Voorhees, supported by the Episcopal Church since 1924, changed its mission during the first half of the twentieth century and in 1962 became Voorhees College.

DENMARK TECHNICAL COLLEGE

1126 Soloman Blatt Blvd, Denmark

The General Assembly of the State of South Carolina authorized the establishment of Denmark Technical College in 1947, and the college began operation on March 1, 1948 as the Denmark Branch of the South Carolina Trade School System.

In 1969 the control of Denmark Area Trade School was transferred to the South Carolina Advisory Committee for Technical Training. During the same year, the name of the college was changed to Denmark Technical Education Center. In 1979 the institution was accredited by the Southern Association of College and Schools and assumed its present designation as Denmark Technical College. Since 1948 the college has experienced significant growth and now takes pride in the fact that it has become a comprehensive two-year college which offers a broad range of programs and services. The college is located in a small city of approximately 5,000 citizens. The campus stands on 53 beautifully landscaped acres of land located about 50 miles south of Columbia, 85 miles northeast of Charleston, and 50 miles east of Augusta, GA.

The college's primary service area is comprised of Bamberg, Barnwell, and Allendale counties with a legislated mandate to serve students throughout the state. As an open-door institution, the college provides affordable, post-secondary education culminating in associate degrees, diplomas, or certificates, to citizens from diverse educational and socioeconomic backgrounds.

BRAINERD INSTITUTE

115 Marquis Street, Chester

This institute grew out of an 1866 school for freedmen. It became Brainerd Institute in 1868 when the Board of Missions of the Presbyterian Church in New York appointed Rev. Samuel Loomis to help establish churches and schools among the Black population near Chester. At first an elementary school, Brainerd grew to ten grades by 1913 and was a four-year high school by the 1930s. Renamed Brainerd Junior College about 1935, it emphasized teacher training until it closed in 1939.

The vision of the Brainerd Institute Heritage is to preserve and share the academic, artistic, and cultural contributions of Brainerd Institute. The site is currently home to Workshops in Open Fields, a program created by Dr. Vivian Ayers Allen to foster and promote preschool literacy.

METROPOLITAN AME

182 York Street, Chester

This congregation, organized in 1866 as a brush arbor near Mt. Zion Church, was one of the first African Methodist Episcopal Zion (AMEZ) churches established in South Carolina after the Civil War. The first wooden structure was built by the members in 1874. It was replaced by the current brick Romanesque Revival building under the direction of self-trained architect Fred Landers in 1913. Metropolitan is a historic property in the City of Chester Historic District. The Chester Historic District was listed on the National Register of Historic Places in 1972.

DIZZY GILLESPIE HOMESITE PARK

344 Huger Street, Cheraw

John Birks "Dizzy" Gillespie (1917-1993), a founder of modern jazz, was born in a house on this site. He lived here until 1935 when his family moved to Philadelphia. An innovative trumpeter and bandleader, he was known for his bent horn, bulging cheeks, humor, and showmanship. With compositions such as "Groovin' High," "Salt Peanuts," and "A Night in Tunisia," Gillespie helped create the bebop style that revolutionized jazz in the 1940s. He played concerts in dozens of countries, earning him the nickname "the Ambassador of Jazz." He received both the National Medal of Arts and the Kennedy Center Honors. A seven-foot bronze statue of Gillespie playing his trademark bent horn stands in Cheraw's Town Green on Market Street.

Dizzy Gillespie Homesite Park

COULTER ACADEMY

353 Second Street, Cheraw

Organized in 1881, this Negro Presbyterian (USA) school was founded by Rev. J. P. Crawford with support from Mrs. C. E. Coulter from whom it received its name. Rev. G. W. Long was academy president from 1908 until 1943, and Coulter offered junior college credit, 1933-1947. The academy merged with the public school system in 1949.

MT. CARMEL AME ZION CHURCH AND CAMPGROUND

4400 Mt. Carmel Road, Cauthen's Crossroads

Isom Caleb Clinton (1830-1904), a former slave, helped establish Mt. Carmel African Methodist Episcopal Zion Church and its campground (circa 1870). The campground was the site of meetings held every September. The church is located on the southern side of the campground, and the church graveyard is located on the northern side. It includes the grave of Frederick Albert Clinton (1834-1890), younger brother of Isom Clinton. Frederick Clinton was instrumental in the founding and growth of Mt. Carmel and was also involved in politics, serving in the South Carolina Senate from 1870 to 1877.

TRINITY AME

39 West Rigby Street, Manning

This church was founded soon after the Civil War by 50 freedpeople who held their first services in a stable donated to them by S. A. Rigby. In 1869 the church trustees bought a half-acre lot for a school and in 1870 they bought a one-acre lot for a sanctuary. The first church here, a frame building, was completed in 1874. A second building was destroyed by fire in 1895. The present building, also of frame construction, was built in that year and later covered in brick veneer. The Central South Carolina Conference of the AME Church was organized here in 1921.

MT. ZION AME

6547 M W Rickenbacker Rd, Summerton

Organized about 1865, this congregation held its early services in a nearby brush arbor and built a permanent sanctuary here soon afterwards. The original building was torn down in 1918 and the lumber used to construct the new one, which still stands. Church member I. S. Hilton served as principal of Mt. Zion School, which once stood nearby. From 1948 to 1954 the church hosted meetings on the desegregation of public schools, and member Levi Pearson was the plaintiff in Pearson v. County Board of Education (1948), which led to the landmark decision in Brown v. Board of Education (1954).

EBENEZER BAPTIST CHURCH

105 Dinkins Street, Manning

This church was founded about 1869 by Mary Scott "Aunt Mary" Harvin and held its first services in a nearby brush arbor. In 1881 church trustees purchased a one-half acre lot here for $35. The present building, constructed in 1901, was described as "enlarged and beautified on a very modern style" when two towers, a gallery, and anterooms were added in 1912. On April 20, 1949, plaintiffs in the suit that became *Briggs* v. *Elliott* met here. This was one of five school desegregation cases that the US Supreme Court decided as *Brown* v. *Board of Education* (1954).

St. Mark AME Church

ST. MARK AME CHURCH

2 1st Street, Summerton

Organized in 1885 from Liberty Hill AME Church, the first St. Mark AME Church was a frame building. In 1905 the congregation purchased a church from the Presbyterian Church and moved it to the site. This building was struck by lightning and burned in 1915. The church rebuilt the present building that same year. St. Mark AME often served as a meeting place for African American students and parents of Summerton, including the petitioners in the *Briggs* v. *Elliott* case as they fought for equal access to education.

THE BRIGGS HOME

1088 Hill Street, Summerton

Harry and Eliza Briggs were the lead plaintiffs in *Briggs* v. *Elliott*. Their son, Harry Jr., attended Scott's Branch School in Summerton. The case was consolidated with other school segregation challenges by the NAACP into the *Brown* v. *Board of Education* suit, which the Supreme Court decided in favor of the plaintiffs in 1954. The Briggses faced severe retaliation from local whites, including the loss of their jobs and home, and the family fled north. Mrs. Briggs eventually returned to Clarendon County many years later.

LIBERTY HILL AME

2310 Liberty Hill Road, Manning

In 1867 Thomas and Margaret Briggs gave four acres of land to this congregation. The present building was completed in 1905 and was later veneered in brick. Meetings held here in the 1940s and 1950s led to local court cases that helped bring about the US Supreme Court's landmark ruling desegregating public schools. Nineteen members of this congregation were plaintiffs in the case of *Briggs* v. *Elliott*, heard in US District Court in Charleston in 1952. Although the three-judge panel refused to abolish racial segregation in South Carolina schools, a dissenting opinion influenced the Supreme Court's decision in *Brown* v. *Board of Education* (1954).

BUTLER SCHOOL

1103 S. 6th Street, Hartsville

Butler School, located on this site since 1921, was the second school to serve Hartsville's Black community. Known as the Darlington County Training School until 1939, it was renamed for Rev. Henry H. Butler, its principal from 1909 to 1946. The first building on this site burned in 1961; extant buildings date from 1936 to the mid-1960s. Butler School was a junior high and high school when it was closed in 1982. Alumni formed the Butler Heritage Foundation, which acquired and renovated the historic campus and reopened it as a community center. A popular homecoming, Butler Heritage Week, is held each July.

MAYO HIGH SCHOOL

405 Chestnut Street, Darlington

Today the Mayo High School of Math, Science, and Technology in Darlington is a highly ranked magnet school. However, when it was built around 1950, it served Darlington's African American population during the height of segregation. The school was named for Dr. Dwight Mayo, a minister and educator who sought to educate African American children here as early as 1889.

BETTIS ACADEMY

78 Nicholson Road, Trenton

Founded by the Mount Canaan Educational Association, a cooperative venture of area Baptist churches, Bettis Academy operated here from the early 1880s until 1952. The curriculum included the standard academic subjects as well as religion, teacher education, and vocational training. It eventually grew to a student body of more than 1,000 and added a junior college on a 350-acre campus. South Carolina's school equalization campaign forced its closure in 1952. Today only three buildings remain—Alexander Bettis Community Library (1938), the Classroom Building (circa 1935), and Biddle Hall (1942)—and a large county park occupies part of the site.

CAMP WELFARE

5200 Camp Welfare Road, Winnsboro

Affiliated with the African Methodist Episcopal Church, Camp Welfare has hosted an annual camp meeting, held each August since at least 1876. The site includes some 100 simple cabins, called tents, arranged in a double U shape. The older tents, probably constructed around 1900, are wood frame, while some of the newer ones are constructed of concrete block. Many of the families have continued to attend through several generations, passing their tents down through the family. The focal point of the site is the "arbor," originally a true brush arbor and now a rough gable-roofed, wooden shelter with benches where worship services are held.

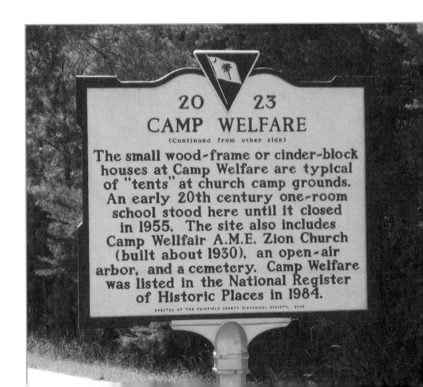

RONALD E. MCNAIR LIFE HISTORY CENTER

235 East Main Street, Lake City

Opened in 2011, the Ronald E. McNair Life History Center is a museum that pays tribute to the life of Dr. McNair, a Lake City-born astronaut and physicist who died in the 1986 Challenger Space Shuttle explosion. Through moving photography and artifacts, the museum tells the story of Dr. McNair from his childhood to his death. A renowned physicist who was a pioneer in the field of lasers, as well as an accomplished saxophonist, Dr. McNair from an early age showed a fascination with science and math and overcame the discrimination of the 1960s South to pursue those interests. Housed in Lake City's old public library, the museum sits next to Dr. McNair's gravesite along with a statue and square erected in his honor. *Open Wed. and Sat. 11 a.m. to 2 p.m., and Sun. 2 p.m. to 4 p.m. Closed all other days.*

RONALD E.
McNAIR

HISTORIC JAMESTOWN

E. Old Marion Highway near Jamestown Road, Mars Bluff

Determined to own his own land rather than to rent or sharecrop, the formerly enslaved Ervin James (1815-1872) bought a 105-acre tract here in 1870. His five sons and a son-in-law later divided the tract into individual farms, and other area families purchased additional land, creating a rural community of some 250 residents that flourished for 70 years. Among its institutions were Jamestown Cemetery, Summerville Methodist Church (now Bowers Chapel United Methodist Church), established about 1880, and an elementary school founded in 1926. Only one of the settlement's original houses remains. A large family reunion, with educational programs open to the public, is held each July.

Pictured at right: Jamestown Foundation founder Terry James, who is a descendant of Ervin James.

Historic Jamestown

THE ASSASSINATION OF FRAZIER BAKER

Deep River and Church streets, Lake City

In 1897 local Black schoolteacher Frazier Baker was appointed postmaster of Lake City by the new Republican administration of President William McKinley. With a new state constitution just adopted to remove Blacks from politics, many white South Carolinians were incensed at such appointments. On the night of February 21, 1898, after a campaign of harassment and arson, a mob set fire to the temporary post office on this site and shot at Baker and his family as they attempted to flee, killing him and an infant daughter and injuring the rest. A subsequent federal case against 11 defendants resulted in a mistrial.

HISTORIC DOWNTOWN AFRICAN AMERICAN HISTORIC DISTRICT

200 and 300 blocks of North Dargan Street, Florence

The 200 and 300 blocks of North Dargan Street were once the center of a thriving African American business district in Florence. A number of Black-owned businesses operated here, including restaurants, barber shops, funeral parlors, and pharmacies. These businesses provided services to African American customers who were often denied access to white-owned businesses. By the first decades of the 20th century, North Florence had become the principal African American residential district as patterns of racial segregation became more fixed. The shops located on North Dargan Street, just north of the Atlantic Coast Line Railroad, served the predominantly African American residents who lived and worked here.

BONDS CONWAY HOUSE

811 Fair Street, Camden

Bonds Conway, born a slave in Virginia in 1763, was brought to Kershaw County in 1792 by his owner, Peter Conway, who allowed him to hire himself out and earn money. He purchased his own freedom in 1793. Thereafter he worked as a skilled carpenter and also began to purchase land in Camden. By the time of his death, Conway owned land extending through the center of town. He built this house on that property (circa 1812). In the 1970s the Kershaw County Historical Society purchased the house, moved it to its present location, and restored it. The house is included in the Camden Historic District and is open to the public on a limited basis. *By appointment only.*

PEARL FRYAR'S GARDEN

145 Broad Acres Road, Bishopville

Two acres of meticulously sculpted plants include graceful arches, spirals, geometrics, abstract shapes and fantasies—all the work of internationally recognized South Carolina topiary artist Pearl Fryar. The garden has been featured on national television shows and in several international publications. In 2006 the award-winning documentary *A Man Named Pearl* was released. Today, visitors from around the world come to see Pearl's beautiful and fascinating horticultural sculpture garden. Park across the street and stroll the outdoor garden at your leisure. If Pearl is in the garden, he is happy to say hello. *Please call ahead to schedule group tours. Online pre-registration is required for each garden. Open Tues. through Sat., 10 a.m. to 4 p.m.*

ISAAC WOODARD MARKER

Corner of W. Church and Fulmer Streets, Batesburg-Leesville

Sergeant Isaac Woodard, a Black soldier, was removed from a bus in Batesburg and arrested on Feb. 12, 1946, after a dispute with the bus driver. Woodard was beaten and blinded by a town police officer, charged, and convicted for being "drunk and disorderly." The incident led Harry Truman to form a Council on Civil Rights and issue Executive Order 9981, which desegregated the US Armed Forces in 1948. The police officer was charged with violating Woodard's civil rights but was acquitted by an all-white jury. The result troubled the presiding judge, J. Waties Waring, who would go on to issue landmark civil rights rulings, including a dissent in *Briggs* v. *Elliott* (1952), which became a model for *Brown* v. *Board of Education* (1954). In 2018, a judge, on the town's motion, expunged Woodard's conviction.

PEOPLES HOSPITAL

1719 Vincent Street, Newberry

Peoples Hospital, the first and only hospital for African Americans in the county from 1937 until Newberry County Memorial Hospital was desegregated in 1952, stood here until 1970. It was founded by Dr. Julian Edward Grant (1900-1997), who practiced medicine in Newberry County for more than 50 years. Grant, a native of Marlboro County, was educated at Claflin University and Meharry Medical College in Nashville, TN, before moving to Newberry in 1930. The building, later the Vincent Street Community Center after the hospital closed in 1952, was demolished in 1970 to build Vincent Street Park.

HOPE ROSENWALD SCHOOL

1971 Hope Station Road, Pomaria

The two-acre lot for this original Rosenwald School was donated by James H. Hope, Mary Hope Hipp, and John J. Hope. James H. Hope, then South Carolina Superintendent of Education, was its longest-serving head, 1922-1947. The school closed in 1954. In 1958 it was sold to the Jackson Community Center and Cemetery Association, comprised of nine members of the adjacent Street Paul AME Church. That group maintained the school for many years. It became the Hope Community Center in 2006.

HOWARD JUNIOR HIGH SCHOOL

431 Shiloh Street, Prosperity

Howard Junior High School (also known as Shiloh School) was built on the site of an earlier school constructed by the Shiloh AME Church. This one-story, wood-frame building was constructed in 1924-25 with matching funds from the Julius Rosenwald Fund. The Howard Junior High School, which was built according to plans developed by the Rosenwald Fund, had four classrooms and featured the rows of large windows typical of Rosenwald Schools. In the 1930s two additional classrooms were added to the south end of the original structure.

SOUTH CAROLINA STATE UNIVERSITY / ORANGEBURG MASSACRE MONUMENT

300 College Street NE, Orangeburg

South Carolina State University was founded in 1896 as the Colored Normal, Industrial, Agricultural & Mechanical College of South Carolina, with its origins in the Morrill Land Grant Acts of 1862 and 1890 providing for land-grant colleges. Intended "for the best education of the hand, head and heart of South Carolina's young manhood and womanhood of the Negro race," it became SC State College in 1954 and SC State University in 1992. SC State has been called "at least symbolically, the most important educational institution in Black Carolina since its founding." Between 1917 and 1949 South Carolina State was able to improve its physical plant in spite of inadequate state funding. The buildings constructed on campus during this period were usually designed by faculty of the college and often built by students.

Students also were active in the civil rights movement of the 1950s and 60s, taking part in sit-ins and the Orangeburg Movement of 1963-64, seeking desegregation of downtown businesses. In 1968 South Carolina State students' protest of the segregation of the All Star Bowling Lanes turned into tragedy. During a confrontation between angry students and local law enforcement, state highway patrolmen fired into a group of students, killing three of them and wounding 28 others. A monument to the memory of Henry Smith, Samuel Hammond, and Delano Middleton was erected. In February of 2022, on the 54th anniversary of the Orangeburg Massacre, South Carolina State University dedicated bronze busts of the three young men killed by law enforcement during the civil rights protest.

nd, Jr.

Delano B. Middleton

Cleveland Sellers Jr., who was among those wounded in the Orangeburg Massacre, stands at the Smith Hammond Middleton Monument dedicated in remembrance of the three men who were killed.

ORANGEBURG CITY CEMETERY

300 College Street NE, Orangeburg

The Orangeburg Cemetery Association purchased this land in 1888. When it was chartered in 1889, the Orangeburg City Cemetery became the first non-church-owned cemetery for African Americans in Orangeburg. Many prominent African American residents of Orangeburg are buried here, including Johnson C. Whittaker, one of the first African American cadets at West Point (and father of Miller F. Whittaker), and Robert Wilkinson, a president of South Carolina State.

TRINITY UNITED METHODIST CHURCH

185 Boulevard Street NE, Orangeburg

This African American church, established in 1866, built its first sanctuary four blocks SE in 1870. Construction began on this sanctuary in 1928 and was completed in 1944. Trinity, headquarters for the Orangeburg Movement during the 1960s, hosted many civil rights meetings and rallies attended by leaders such as Dr. Martin Luther King Jr., Roy Wilkins, and Thurgood Marshall.

CLAFLIN UNIVERSITY HISTORIC DISTRICT

400 Magnolia Street, Orangeburg

In 1869 Methodist ministers from the North who had come to South Carolina as missionaries to former slaves established Claflin University. The school was named in honor of the family of Lee Claflin, a wealthy Methodist layman of Massachusetts. In addition to Northern missionaries, the board of trustees included prominent Black South Carolinians. Although it was chartered as a university, in the early years, Claflin, of necessity, provided a basic grammar school education for the freedmen. In the early 20th century, Claflin provided hundreds of students from all parts of the state with a high school education. The name of the school was changed from Claflin University to Claflin College in 1914. In 1922 Dr. J.B. Randolph became the first African American president of Claflin. In the following years, as public education improved somewhat, the number of college students increased and the high school and grammar school courses were discontinued. Numerous graduates achieved prominence in medicine, the ministry, and other professional fields. The education of teachers was a primary goal of the school, which provided teachers for public schools throughout the state. Historic buildings on the Claflin campus reflect the development of the school in the last years of the 19th and the first two decades of the 20th centuries. These include Lee Library (1898), Tingley Memorial Hall (1908), Trustee Hall (circa 1910), Wilson Hall (1913), and the Dining Hall (1913). Lee Library and Tingley Memorial Hall were designed by William Wilson Cooke, superintendent of vocational training at Claflin and a pioneer African American architect in the nation.

AFRICAN AMERICAN MONUMENT ON THE SC STATEHOUSE GROUNDS

1100 Gervais Street, Columbia

This monument illustrates the story of African Americans in South Carolina from the 16th century to the present. Among the 12 scenes carved into the monument are images of an enslaved family on the auction block, freedmen celebrating the Emancipation Proclamation, and unnamed African American pioneers in a variety of disciplines. Four rubbing stones representing the regions where Africans were captured and sold into slavery—Senegal, Sierra Leone, the Republic of Congo, and Ghana—are also located at the base.

RANDOLPH CEMETERY

Western terminus of Elmwood Avenue, Columbia

Randolph Cemetery was established by a group of African American civic leaders in 1872 and expanded in 1899. They named the cemetery for Benjamin Franklin Randolph, an African American who was assassinated by white men while campaigning for the Republican Party in Abbeville County in 1868. It is not clear whether Randolph was buried on the property since the cemetery was established after his death, but a monument to his memory is located at the entrance. The cemetery also includes the graves of eight other African American members of the SC General Assembly and numerous other leaders of Columbia's African American community in the late 19th and early 20th centuries.

ALLEN UNIVERSITY HISTORIC DISTRICT

1530 Harden Street, Columbia

Originally founded in Cokesbury in 1870 as Payne Institute, the school was relocated to Columbia by AME leadership nearly a decade later. It was renamed Allen University in honor of Bishop Richard Allen, the founder of the African Methodist Episcopal Church. The campus features five historic buildings: Arnett Hall, named for Rev. Benjamin W. Arnett; Coppin Hall; the Canteen; Chappelle Administration Building, named for William David Chappelle, a former president; and the Joseph Simon Flipper Library.

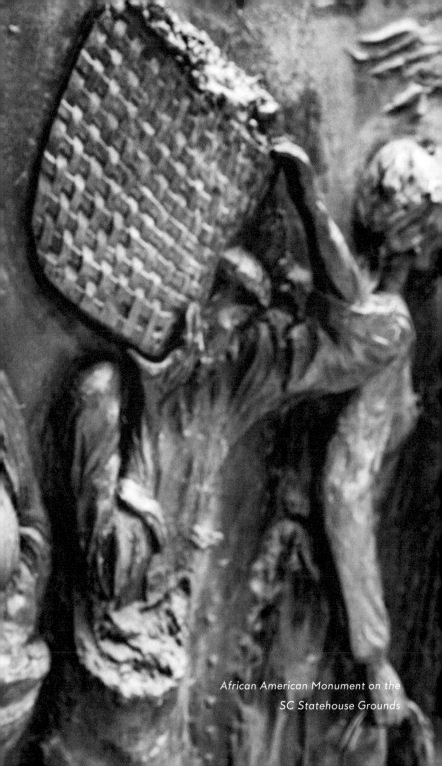

African American Monument on the
SC Statehouse Grounds

MUSEUM OF THE RECONSTRUCTION ERA AT THE WOODROW WILSON FAMILY HOME

1705 Hampton Street, Columbia

The Woodrow Wilson Family Home: A Museum of Reconstruction enjoys the dual distinction of being the nation's only museum dedicated to interpreting the post-Civil War Reconstruction period and South Carolina's only remaining presidential site. Through exhibit galleries, hands-on interactive displays, and audio and video components, this award-winning museum explores the racial, social, and political landscape of Columbia and Richland County from 1865 through 1877, an era in which formerly enslaved African Americans negotiated the opportunities and obstacles faced as new citizens of the United States.

Completed in 1871, this Italian villa-style residence was home to a 14-year-old boy—the future 28th United States President—named "Tommy" Woodrow Wilson. During the height of Reconstruction, Woodrow Wilson's parents built this house, the only one they would ever own. Although the home has changed hands many times since the teenaged future president lived here, it stands as a reminder of the complicated racial history of one of the most misrepresented and misunderstood periods of American history.

The museum is operated by Historic Columbia and tours of the Museum of the Reconstruction Era at the Woodrow Wilson Family Home are available Wednesday-Saturday at 10:30 a.m. and Sunday at 1:30 p.m. Tickets can be purchased at the Gift Shop at Robert Mills, located at 1616 Blanding Streeet.

1963 USC DESEGREGATION
COMMEMORATIVE GARDEN

1501 Pendleton Street, Columbia

On September 11, 1963, Robert Anderson, Henrie Montieth, and James Solomon became the first African American students since Reconstruction to enroll at the University of South Carolina. The 1963 USC Desegregation Commemorative Garden marks the 50th anniversary of the historic day when the color barrier was broken at the state's flagship university. Inspired by themes of diversity, equality, and transformation, the garden offers symbolic focal points including brick pathways and three juniper topiaries created by Pearl Fryar, the nationally renowned topiary artist of Bishopville. A granite monument features the poem, "The Irresistable Ones," written by 2011 National Book Award winner and USC professor Nikki Finney. The garden offers a quiet place for reflection and meaningful conversation.

MANN-SIMONS SITE

1403 Richland Street, Columbia

The Mann-Simon Site takes guests on a journey through the challenges, adversity, and perseverance of one African American family who lived on the property for nearly 130 years. The exhibits, which debuted in the fall of 2016, explore the role race played in shaping the capital city—from antebellum Columbia, to the Civil War and Reconstruction, to the Jim Crow era and into the early civil rights years. Today, the site is operated as a house museum by Historic Columbia. *Tours of the Mann-Simons Site are available Wed. to Sat. at 1:30 p.m. and Sunday at 3 p.m.*

RICHARD T. GREENER MEMORIAL

1322 Green Street, Columbia

This statue is dedicated to the memory of Richard Theodore Greener (1844-1922), a professor of philosophy, scholar, librarian, and law graduate of the Reconstruction-era University of South Carolina. Born in Philadelphia and raised in Boston, Greener attended preparatory school at Oberlin College and Phillips Academy. He was the first African American to graduate from Harvard College and the first African American faculty member at the University of South Carolina, from 1873-1877. He later served as the Dean of the Howard University Law School, as Secretary of the Grant Monument Association, and as a US consular officer to Vladivostok, Russia.

ZION BAPTIST CHURCH

801 Washington Street, Columbia

Zion Baptist Church first organized in 1865 and met in a humble dwelling on Gadsden Street. The congregation moved to this site in 1871. The current sanctuary, the second on this spot, was built in 1916. In 1930 Dr. Matilda Evans, the first African American woman to have a medical practice in the state, started a free clinic in the basement of the church. On March 2, 1961 more than 200 African American students met at Zion Baptist before their march to the State House to protest racial segregation. The US Supreme Court later overturned the convictions of those students arrested during the march.

MODJESKA MONTEITH SIMKINS HOUSE

2025 Marion Street, Columbia

The Modjeska Monteith Simkins House, built between 1890 and 1895, was home to Modjeska Monteith Simkins, considered the matriarch of South Carolina's civil and human rights movement. Simkins was a founder of the South Carolina Conference of the NAACP. As the secretary of the conference, Simkins hosted many meetings and planning sessions at her home for local and national civil rights leaders and NAACP lawyers, including Thurgood Marshall during the *Brown v. Board* of *Education* trial. Today, the site is operated as a house museum by Historic Columbia. The house is available for private, guided tours for small groups. *For any additional availability or to schedule your group, call (803) 252-1770 x 23 or email reservations@historiccolumbia.org.*

I've always had hope in youn~~~
and I've always worked w~~~

MODJESKA MONTEITH SIMKINS

RISE UP

~~~hilo~~~ ~~~~~~~~~~~s been,
~~~vel~~~ ~~~dy~~~ that's going my

MODJESKA MONTEITH SIMKINS, IN~~~

~~~re has always feared

~~~d white masses.

MODJESKA MONTEITH SIMKINS,
INTERVIEW, 1976

Thank God
for Mississippi
It keeps
~~~~~~~~~~~

DIDNT COME
S FAR TO ONLY
ME THIS FAR

~~~ Time

| ~~~of an~~~ | Passage of an anti-poll tax law | Passage of a $0.90 minimum wage law | Passage of a law establishing national health insurance | Passage of a law establishing fortes bargaining for workers in domestic, casual, and agricultural empl~~~ | Passage of a law providing federal aid to education |

as Vidas
NEGRAS
IPORTAN!

Modjeska Monteith Simkins House

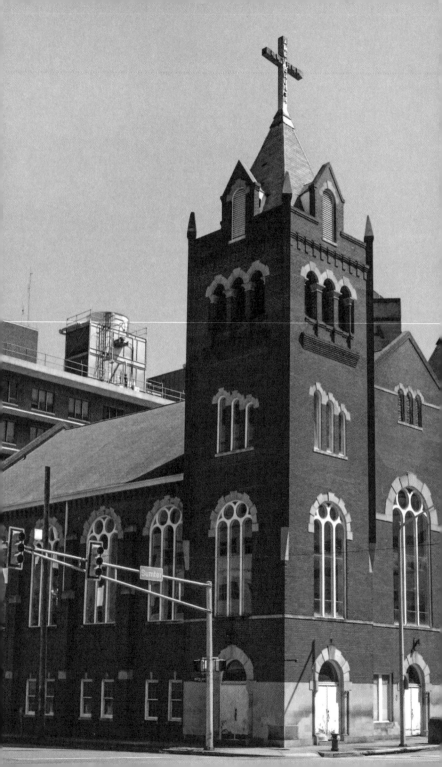

BETHEL AME CHURCH

1528 Sumter Street, Columbia

Founded by freedmen after the Civil War, Bethel AME Church relocated to Sumter Street in 1921. John Anderson Lankford, one of the first registered Black architects in the United States, designed the Romanesque Revival brick structure. Bethel boasted one of the largest Black congregations in Columbia throughout the 20th century. The building was the site of numerous mass meetings and planning sessions during the 1960s civil rights movement.

HARRIET CORNWELL TOURIST HOUSE

1713 Wayne Street, Columbia

The Harriet M. Cornwell Tourist House was listed in the National Register as part of the Multiple Property Submission "Segregation in Columbia." From circa 1940 to circa 1960 during the era of segregation, the Harriet M. Cornwell Tourist Home served as a place where African Americans could find lodging and one meal a day. While no sign advertised the house as a tourist home for Blacks, the house and its address were advertised nationally in *The Negro Travelers' Green Book* and the *International Travelers' Green Book*.

BIRTHPLACE OF MARY MCLEOD BETHUNE

Intersection of Highways 154 and US 76, Mayesville

Born on July 10, 1875, near Mayesville, Mary McLeod Bethune devoted her life to the advancement of her race. She was one of the first pupils and later taught at Mayesville Mission School, located 50 yards west of this marker. Bethune founded and directed educational policy at Bethune-Cookman College, a historically Black college in Daytona Beach, Florida. She also founded the National Council of Negro Women in 1935. In addition, Bethune was a member of the"Black Cabinet," a select group of Black appointees to New Deal agencies who advised President Roosevelt on racial matters. She also was a consultant during the drafting of the United Nations Charter. This noted humanitarian and educator died on May 18, 1955, and is buried at Bethune-Cookman College.

Historic Brattonsville

HISTORIC BRATTONSVILLE

1444 Brattonsville Road, McConnells

Historic Brattonsville presents the history of the Scots-Irish and African Americans in the South Carolina upcountry largely through preserving and interpreting the story of the Bratton community. This site has more than 30 historic structures from the 1760s to the late 19th century, including an original brick slave cabin. This site celebrates the rich heritage of African Americans in an annual program entitled "By the Sweat of Our Brows." During this powerful program, visitors have the opportunity to learn about the enslaved community of Brattonsville as well as meet and hear from descendants of those who were once enslaved here. *Open Open Tues. through Sat., 10 a.m. to 5 p.m., and Sunday from 1 p.m. to 5 p.m. Group visits involving 15 or more people must be scheduled in advance. Call 803.981.9182.*

A brand-new exhibit is located in the hallway next to Kounter at 135 E. Main Street. The Jail, No Bail: How 30 Days Impacted the Civil Rights Movement exhibit captures the unique role their protest played in the 1960s civil rights movement. This exhibition tells the story of a group of individuals who together altered the course of civil rights. Hours: Tues. to Fri. 10 a.m. to 4 p.m. and Sat. to Sun. 11 a.m. to 4 p.m.

MCCRORY'S FIVE AND DIME

137 E. Main Street, Rock Hill

Inspired by the bravery of the Greensboro Four, roughly 100 Black students from Friendship Junior College in Rock Hill participated in the first sit-in demonstrations in South Carolina on February 12, 1960. The students sat down at lunch counters in downtown drug and department stores such as Woolworth's, Good Drug Company, J.L. Phillips "RexAll" Drug Company, and McCrory's Five and Dime, just yards from where this historical marker is located. Sit-in demonstrations and other protests against segregation continued for over a year.

On January 31, 1961, nine students from Friendship Junior College and CORE organizer Thomas Gaither were arrested when they refused to leave McCrory's after being denied service. All but one of those arrested refused to post bail, opting instead to serve time. Several were sent to the York County Prison Farm for hard labor and subjected to solitary confinement. Organizers of the Freedom Rides and later protest campaigns adopted the "Jail, No Bail" strategy to pressure city governments to end segregation.

In 2015 Judge John C. Hayes III overturned the convictions of the Friendship Nine stating: "We cannot rewrite history, but we can right history." The former McCrory's building has been named as a stop on the United States Civil Rights Trail and the National Parks Service African American Civil Rights Network. Today you can view the lunch counter's stools and original surface, protected by a special epoxy.

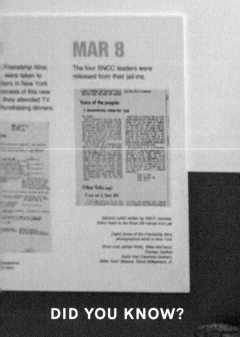

MAR 8

The four SNCC leaders were
released from their jail-ins.

Voice of the people:

Other folks say:

DID YOU KNOW?

After McCrory's closed its doors in
1997, the original lunch counter was
at risk of being sold and removed.
A local organizing committee raised
$30,000 from the Museums of York
County and the City of Rock Hill to
preserve the counter. A base was built
around the original counter, and the
stools and footrails were restored
and remained in the restaurant, now
called Kounter.

EMMETT SCOTT SCHOOL

801 Crawford Road, Rock Hill

This school, founded in 1920, was the first public school for Blacks in Rock Hill. Named for Emmett J. Scott (1873-1957), a prominent educator who was then secretary of Howard University, Emmett Scott School included all 12 grades until 1956 and was a junior high and high school from 1956 until South Carolina schools were desegregated in 1970. The original two-story frame school was demolished in 1952. This property is owned by the City of Rock Hill and has been a neighborhood recreation center since the school closed in 1970.

LIBERTY HILL ROSENWALD SCHOOL

3071 S. Anderson Road, Catawba

The Catawba Rosenwald School was built in 1924-25 to serve the African American community in southeastern York County. It was known as the Catawba School on official lists of Rosenwald schools, but is generally known as the Liberty Hill School locally because of its association with Liberty Hill Missionary Baptist Church nearby. It was one of 20 schools built in York County with funds from the Rosenwald program between 1917 and 1932. Of these schools, only two, the Catawba Rosenwald School and the Carroll Rosenwald School, are known to be extant. The Catawba School was built according to Rosenwald Plan #20 as a two-teacher rural school.

Pictured above: Pearline Feely Barber

THE CARROLL SCHOOL

4789 Mobley Store Road, Rock Hill

The Carroll School is a three-classroom frame school. The school served the African American community in the Ogden area of York County from its opening in 1929 until 1954, when it was closed. It was listed on the National Register under Criterion A (Ethnic Heritage: Black; Education) and Criterion C (Architecture). The Carroll School was located across the road from New Zion Baptist Church and was associated with the church in many activities. Records at the Rock Hill School District office show that

in the early 1950s, plans to consolidate schools were underway
to provide better and larger facilities for the African American
students. The Carroll School closed in 1954 and students were
transferred to a newly consolidated African American school, the
Fairview School. In 2001 an effort was begun by Rock Hill School
District #3 to restore the building and use it as a site for an
in-district field trip for all fifth grade students in the District.

The Penn Center

THE LOWCOUNTRY

International African American History Museum

SUGGESTED DAY TRIP

9 A.M. MITCHELVILLE FREEDOM PARK

229 Beach City Road, Hilton Head Island (843-255-7301)

Time at site: 1 hour

Drive time to St. Helena Island: 45 minutes

10:15 A.M. GRAND ARMY OF THE REPUBLIC HALL

706 Newcastle Street, Beaufort

Time at site: 30 minutes.

11:30 A.M. RECONSTRUCTION ERA NATIONAL MONUMENT

706 Craven Street, Beaufort (843-962-0039)

Time at site: 30 minutes

12 P.M. TABERNACLE BAPTIST CHURCH

901 Craven Street, Beaufort (843-524-0376)

Time at site: 15 minutes

Drive time to St. Helena Island: 30 minutes

12:30 P.M. LUNCH

Gullah Grub (large groups must call in advance)

877 Sea Island Parkway, St. Helena Island (843-838-3841)

1:30 P.M. PENN CENTER / RECONSTRUCTION ERA NATIONAL MONUMENT

16 Penn Center Circle West, St. Helena Island (843-838-2432)

Time at site: 2 hours.

PENN CENTER / RECONSTRUCTION ERA NATIONAL MONUMENT

16 Penn Center Circle West, St. Helena Island

First known as Penn School, this important African American cultural center was founded in 1862 by Northern missionaries and abolitionists who came to South Carolina after the capture of the Sea Islands by Union troops. It was the first school founded in the South specifically for the education of African American students. They named the center after their home state.

The 47-acre site and its collection of historic buildings have long been venues for education and the preservation and interpretation of sea island culture. In the 1960s Penn Center served as a strategy center for the Southern Christian Leadership Conference and Dr. Martin Luther King Jr., who came here five times between 1963 and 1967. Other critical meetings occurred here for the Congress of Racial Equality (CORE), the Student Non-Violent Coordinating Committee (SNCC), and other civil rights organizations.

More recently, Penn Center has turned its attention to preserving sea island Gullah culture through various workshops. In January 2017 Penn Center and other historic sites in Beaufort County were declared the nation's first Reconstruction Era National Monument by President Barack Obama. In 2019 the monument was officially recognized as a National Historic Park. *The campus is available for self-guided walking tours. A museum and gift shop are located at 706 Craven Street, Beaufort. Open Tues. through Sat., 10 a.m. to 4 p.m. Closed Sunday and Monday.*

FORMER HOME OF WILLIAM SIMMONS (GULLAH MUSEUM OF HILTON HEAD)

12 Georgianna Drive, Hilton Head Island

This house, built in 1930, is typical in materials and methods of construction of those built on the sea islands from the end of the Civil War to the mid-20th century. It was built on land bought by William Simmons (circa 1835-1922), who was born a slave and served in the 21st US Colored Infantry during the Civil War. His granddaughter, Georgianna Jones Bryan, built this house in 1930 for her brother. It illustrates everyday life and the persistence of Gullah culture in an African American farm community. It was renovated in 2011 as the Gullah Museum of Hilton Head Island. *By appointment only.*

TABERNACLE BAPTIST CHURCH

901 Craven Street, Beaufort

The Tabernacle, a meeting house and lecture room, was built by Beaufort Baptist Church in the 1840s. In 1863 Tabernacle Baptist Church was organized by Solomon Peck of Boston with most of the 500 African American members of the congregation coming from Beaufort Baptist Church. The new congregation acquired this building for their worship services. The church was rebuilt after it was damaged by the hurricane of 1893. A bust of Civil War Hero Robert Smalls is on the church grounds. Tabernacle Baptist Church is included in the Beaufort Historic District.

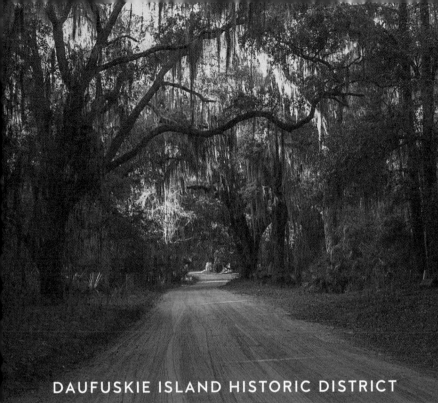

DAUFUSKIE ISLAND HISTORIC DISTRICT

Accessible by ferry from Broad Creek Marina at 18 Simmons Road, Hilton Head Island

The cotton trade spurred the growth of the slave population on Daufuskie Island from 1805-1842, and ruins of slave houses and archaeological sites remain from this period. The island was largely abandoned during the Civil War but many former slaves returned during Reconstruction, reoccupying slave houses and building churches, schools, and meeting places. In the early 20th century, the population swelled to almost 1,000, with oysters, logging, and trucking providing jobs. By the 1940s and 1950s, outside competition had caused many to leave the island and search for jobs elsewhere, leaving the African American population in 2020 at fewer than 20 people.

Descendants of Daufuskie's Gullah people still live on the island. Some historic Gullah cottages are rentable for island vacations.

NATIONAL CEMETERY AND GRAND ARMY HALL

1601 Boundary Street, Beaufort

Although Beaufort's Black military companies remained active after the Civil War, statewide the "Negro militia" rapidly declined during the 19th century. By 1903 the only units left were two companies in Beaufort. Many Black Union veterans lived in the community, and after the war they formed the David Hunter Post #9 of the Grand Army of the Republic, an organization for veterans of the Union Army. Built in 1896, this meeting hall for the post is believed to be the only surviving building in South Carolina associated with the Grand Army of the Republic. It is included in the Beaufort Historic District.

HISTORIC MITCHELVILLE FREEDOM PARK

226 Beach City Road, Hilton Head Island

After Hilton Head's fall to Union forces in 1861, this town was planned for the area's former slaves and named for General Ormsby M. Mitchel. It was developed into neatly arranged streets and one-acre lots. The town had elected officials, a church, laws, taxes, and a school for children, and was home to about 1,500 residents in 1865. The village continued relatively intact until the 1870s and was abandoned by 1890. From the Praise House to the Bateau, Mitchelville features historical exhibits that take visitors back in time.
Open every day, 6 a.m. to 9 p.m.

FIRST AFRICAN BAPTIST CHURCH

70 Beach City Road, Hilton Head Island

This was the church of the town of Mitchelville, a freedmen's village established on Hilton Head Island. The church was founded by US Army Rev. Abraham Murchinson, its first minister, who was formerly enslaved. The church had about 120 members when it was organized in August 1862. It moved to the Chaplin community after the Civil War and was renamed Goodwill Baptist Church. It moved again to its present site in 1898 and was renamed Cross Roads Baptist Church before retaking its original name. The present church was built in 1966.

GARVIN-GARVEY HOUSE

Oyster Factory Park, Bluffton

The Garvin-Garvey House, constructed and owned by formerly enslaved African Americans, is located at the intersection of Bridge Street and Wharf Street within the "Old Town" district of Bluffton. The structure dates to 1870 and is an excellent example of Carolina Lowcountry vernacular architecture of the late-19th century. The building was constructed during the Reconstruction era, a historic period rarely represented architecturally due to the impermanence of the construction methods and materials. *Open Tues. and Thurs., 10 a.m. to 4 p.m.*

COOPER RIVER HISTORIC DISTRICT EXHIBIT (CYPRESS GARDENS)

3030 Cypress Gardens Road, Moncks Corner

The Cooper River Historic District includes approximately 30,020 acres along the East and West branch of the river. The district includes many historical buildings and intact cultural landscapes from the 18th, 19th and 20th centuries. Slaves cleared the forests, managed crops, and performed countless domestic services. Archaeological evidence of slave houses, streets, and settlements provides an insight into the lifeways of enslaved African Americans. Open for tours is Cypress Gardens, originally a part of the 1750 Dean Hall rice plantation that relied on the Cooper River. This site provides evidence of slave labor contributions to the rice plantation economy. *Open 7 days a week, 9 a.m. to 5 p.m.*

DRAYTON HALL

3380 Ashley River Road, Charleston

Since the 1970s, tours of Drayton Hall focused primarily on architecture and the building's white residents. The new tour, which was featured on the front page of Charleston's *Post and Courier*, accentuates Drayton Hall's status as an African American history site dedicated to researching and interpreting that history. It is a social history tour that focuses primarily on the enslaved residents of Drayton Hall. In conjunction, a new self-guided walking tour was created for the grounds of Drayton Hall that provides much more information about enslaved people and their enormous contributions to the development of Charleston. *Open Weds. through Mon., 9 a.m. to 3:30 p.m. Closed Thursdays.*

BENCH BY THE ROAD

1214 Middle Street, Sullivan's Island

Beyond military defense, Fort Moultrie tells the story of Sullivan's Island's role as an entry point and quarantine station for West Africans who were brought to the Carolina colony during the Middle Passage. Historians estimate that slave ships brought 200,000 to 360,000 West Africans into the Charleston harbor until the international slave trade was abolished in 1808. Author Toni Morrison led the effort to place this "Bench by the Road" in 2008 to memorialize this history when no monuments or museums marked it.

THE AVERY RESEARCH CENTER FOR AFRICAN AMERICAN HISTORY AND CULTURE

125 Bull Street, Charleston

In 1978 a group of Avery graduates and friends of Avery organized The Avery Institute of Afro-American History and Culture. Its purpose was to obtain the old Avery Normal School buildings and establish in them an archives and museum dedicated to preserving Afro-American history and culture in the South Carolina Lowcountry.

In 1985 The Avery Research Center for African American History and Culture was established as part of the academic program of the College of Charleston. Despite delays caused by the ravages of Hurricane Hugo, the grand opening of the building took place on October 6, 1990. After twelve years of strenuous effort, the Avery Institute of Afro-American History and Culture saw its dream finally realized.

Today the Avery Institute is a separate non-profit organization and provides support to the Center's programs and operations, as well as assisting the Center in acquiring archival collections. The Avery Research Center is open for scholars, students, and the general public to access the center's archives and to tour the historical site. *Tours begin on the first floor. Admission is free; however, donations are welcomed.*

MAGNOLIA PLANTATION

3550 Ashley River Road, Charleston

The plantation was established in 1676 by Draytons who migrated from Barbados. The family and its descendants prospered from the success of agricultural products cultivated by the family's enslaved population. Since the Civil War, the extensive gardens have drawn patrons regularly to enjoy their breathtaking beauty. It is the oldest public tourist site in the Lowcountry, and the oldest public gardens in America, opening its doors to visitors in 1870. Five restored former slave cabins, occupied from the 1850s-1890s, are the focus of a program that highlights African American life on the property.

Magnolia offers various areas of the plantation for touring every day 9 a.m. to 5 p.m. Adult admission starts at $29.

MORRIS BROWN AME

13 Morris Street, Charleston

Morris Brown AME Church was founded in the era following the American Civil War. The congregation came into being because of the rapid growth of Emanuel AME Church, the first church reestablished in Charleston following the Civil War by Bishop Daniel Alexander Payne. The church is named for Morris Brown, the pastor of the first AME congregation established in Charleston in 1818. That congregation was forced "underground" in 1822 when one of its local clergy, Denmark Vesey, was executed for planning an abortive slave rebellion. Brown fled for his life to Philadelphia and became the second Bishop of the AME Church. The "underground" church continued to meet until it was officially revived by Bishop Payne as Emanuel AME Church in 1865.

SWEETGRASS PAVILION

99 Harry M. Hallman Jr. Boulevard, Mount Pleasant

The Sweetgrass Pavilion is an exceptional special event and meeting space that showcases one of the Lowcountry's largest collections of sweetgrass basket merchandise. Hands-on basket-making classes are often held at the venue. The coiled sweetgrass basket is a historically significant African art that was brought to America in the 17th century by enslaved Africans from the Windward and Rice Coasts of West Africa. These baskets were originally designed as a winnowing tool used in the production and processing of rice. Today, they are popular souvenirs found along the South Carolina coast.

THE SEIZURE OF THE PLANTER

40 East Bay Street, Charleston

Early on May 13, 1862, Robert Smalls (1839-1915), an enslaved harbor pilot aboard the Planter, seized the 149-foot Confederate transport from a wharf just east of here. He and six enslaved crewmen took the vessel before dawn when its captain, pilot, and engineer were ashore. Smalls guided the ship through the channel, past Fort Sumter, and out to sea, delivering it to the federal fleet which was blockading the harbor. Northern and Southern newspapers called this feat "bold" and "daring." Smalls, his crew, a crewman on another ship, and eight other enslaved persons including Smalls' wife, Hannah, and three children won their freedom. Smalls was appointed captain of the USS Planter by a US Army contract in 1863. A native of Beaufort, he was later a state legislator and then a five-term US Congressman. This marker was sponsored by the Historic Charleston Foundation and the African American Historical Alliance in 2012.

THE CIGAR FACTORY

701 E. Bay Street, Charleston

Built circa 1882 and known as "the Cigar Factory," this five-story structure was the commercial site of the Charleston Cotton Mills and produced cigars until 1973. Employing some 1,400 workers in 1945, 900 of whom were African American women, the Cigar Factory workers struck for higher wages and an end to discrimination. Strikers sang the gospel hymn "I'll Overcome Someday." Later this song was revised as "We Shall Overcome," and became one of the most popular Freedom Songs of the Civil Rights Movement.

MCLEOD PLANTATION

325 Country Club Drive, Charleston

McLeod Plantation Historic Site features a plantation house and a fully intact row of extant slave dwellings. In 1860, 74 slaves lived in 26 cabins on this Sea Island cotton plantation. Five of those wood-frame slave cabins remain today. During the Civil War the plantation served as unit headquarters for Confederate forces. When they evacuated Charleston in February 1865, the 54th and 55th Massachusetts Volunteer Regiments and other Union regiments camped on-site. The McLeod Plantation House served as headquarters for the Freedmen's Bureau for the James Island district during Reconstruction. The Sankofa Burial Site of our African Ancestors features nearly 100 graves of former inhabitants. McLeod Plantation offers guided tours about African American life from slavery to freedom. *Open Tues. through Sun., 9 a.m. to 4 p.m.. Admission is $6-$20 per person.*

McLeod Plantation

BOONE HALL

1235 Long Point Road, Mount Pleasant

Nine slave houses still remain at Boone Hall and form one of the few remaining slave streets in the state. The houses date from 1790 to 1810, and two of them display exceptional brickwork and feature diamond shaped patterns unusual in South Carolina. The nine slave houses are survivors of the approximately 27 slave houses at Boone Hall, and the nine survivors are believed to have been for house servants. *Tours of the slave houses are available at Boone Hall Plantation and Gardens Mon. through Sat., 9 a.m. to 5 p.m., and Sun., 12 p.m. to 3 p.m. Admission $12-$26 per person.*

ELIZA'S HOUSE AT MIDDLETON PLACE

4300 Ashley River Road, Charleston

Eliza's House is a small frame building named for Eliza Leach (1891-1986), who worked at Middleton Place for more than 40 years and was the last person to live in the house. It is one of several structures on the grounds that interpret African American life. The original occupants of the house are not known, but in the 1880s it was apparently the home of Ned and Chloe, formerly enslaved by Williams and Susan Middleton. The plantation chapel, a room above a springhouse dairy, was used by enslaved people as a house of worship.

Middleton Place recently produced a documentary film of life on the plantation before and after the Civil War, called "Beyond the Fields—Slavery at Middleton Place." *Open every day from 9 a.m. to 5 p.m. Admission $12-$26 per person.*

DENMARK VESEY HOUSE

56 Bull Street, Charleston

Beginning in December 1821, Vesey and other free blacks met in his home on Sunday evenings to plan a rebellion for the summer of 1822. As the date for the rebellion grew closer, one slave who heard of the plot reported it to his master. Several leaders of the rebellion were arrested, and three men testified against Vesey in exchange for promises of immunity. Vesey and more than 30 others were executed for their roles in the conspiracy. Several important actors in the Denmark Vesey insurrection and trial, both white and Black, lived on or near Bull Street.

SLAVE MART MUSEUM

6 Chalmers Street, Charleston

The Old Slave Mart is the only known extant building used as a slave auction gallery in South Carolina. Once part of a complex, the Slave Mart building is the only structure to remain. When first constructed in 1859, the open ended building was referred to as a shed, and used the walls of the German Fire Hall to its west to support the roof timbers. Slave auctions were held inside. The interior was one large room with a 20-foot ceiling, while the front facade was more impressive with its high arch, octagonal pillars, and a large iron gate. *Open Mon. through Sat., 9 a.m. to 5 p.m. Closed Sundays.*

MOTHER EMANUEL AME

110 Calhoun Street, Charleston

The Mother Emanuel AME Church is a Gothic Revival style church built in 1891. Retaining its original altar, communion rail, pews, and light fixtures, the church is one of only a few unaltered religious interiors in Charleston, especially from the Victorian period. The brick Gothic church with its tall steeple replaced an earlier 1872 church badly damaged by the 1886 earthquake. Today Emanuel is the oldest AME church in the South and houses the oldest Black congregation south of Baltimore.

Over the years, the church has hosted such notable African-American leaders as Booker T. Washington, Dr. Martin Luther King Jr., and the Rev. Wyatt T. Walker.

On June 17, 2015, nine parishioners were shot inside the church by a 21-year-old white supremacist. Those killed were Clementa Pinckney, Cynthia Hurd, DePayne Middleton-Doctor, Sharonda Coleman-Singleton, Susie Jackson, Myra Thompson, Tywanza Sanders, Ethel Lance, and Daniel Simmons. Two years after the tragedy, on June 17, 2017, Emanuel AME announced construction of a memorial at the church to honor the nine victims.

SEASHORE FARMERS' LODGE

NE corner of Sol Legare Road & Old Sol Legare Road, John's Island

This newly-restored lodge in the Sol Legare community reflects the tight-knit community that has existed here since Emancipation. Following the Civil War, formerly enslaved people moved to this area to farm and fish. The men who settled here established a fraternal organization and mutual aid society around 1915 called the Sol Legare Seashore Farmers' Lodge No. 767, affiliated with the International Farmers' Liberty Union Justice. Such organizations were immensely popular with African Americans both prior to the Civil War and afterwards, and many were secret, especially before slaves were freed. Members paid dues, which in turn were used to support each other during financial difficulties. The society served as an insurance policy with a social component. The African Americans here could not obtain true insurance from white business owners, and dues from the Seashore Farmers' Lodge helped families with everything from purchasing seeds and farm equipment to paying medical bills and funeral expenses. Today, it's again a community hub and cultural museum that's open to visitors. *Upon arrival, dial the on-call contact posted at the door.*

Pictured at right: Ernest Parks and Douglas "Hosie" Parks

Seashore Farmer's Lodge

EDISTO ISLAND BAPTIST CHURCH

1644 SC Highway 174, Edisto Island

The original core of Edisto Island Baptist Church was built in 1818 to serve the island's white planters. Enslaved African Americans attended the church with their owners, and the original slave gallery still lines both sides of the sanctuary. After Edisto Island was occupied by Union troops during the Civil War, most of the white plantation families left the island. In 1865 the trustees of the church turned it over to the Black members. Edisto Island Baptist Church has operated as an African American church since that time.

HUTCHINSON HOUSE

7666 Point of Pines Road, Edisto Island

Built by Henry Hutchinson around the time of his marriage to Rosa Swinton in 1885, the Hutchinson House is the oldest intact house identified with the African American community on Edisto Island. Hutchinson was born enslaved in 1860, and according to local tradition, he built and operated the first cotton gin owned by an African American on the island from about 1900-1920. Hutchinson lived here until his death in 1940.

TUSKEGEE AIRMEN MEMORIAL

1359 Tuskegee Airmen Drive, Walterboro

During World War II, the first African Americans in the US Army Air Corps graduated from the Tuskegee Army Flying School in Alabama. From May 1944 to October 1945, some of them took further combat training here, at Walterboro Army Air Field. Several of the earliest "Tuskegee Airmen," who had already won fame in missions in Europe and North Africa, were assigned as combat flight instructors. Trainees here flew the P-39, P-47, and P-40 fighter planes and the B-25 bomber. Officers' quarters and enlisted men's barracks stood just east and just west of this spot, respectively. *Open every day, 8 a.m. to 8 p.m.*

SANDY ISLAND

1998 Sandy Island Road, Pawleys Island

Sandy Island is a Gullah community located on the largest freshwater island in the state of South Carolina. The island is 9,000 acres of prehistoric sand dunes bordered by the Pee Dee and Waccamaw Rivers in Georgetown County, and protected by the Nature Conservancy. The community was founded by a freed slave who had worked on nearby rice plantations. Many of the current residents are his descendants. Because the residents live largely isolated from the influence of the mainland's modern culture, the Gullah way of life is preserved. Some of the intriguing sites on the island include an old schoolhouse, a bed and breakfast called Wilma's Cottage, Pyatt's General Store, and the circa 1880 New Bethel Baptist Church. *The island is accessible only by boat and tours are available only by appointment.*

HOBCAW BARONY

22 Hobcaw Road, Georgetown

Assembled in 1905 to 1907 by nationally prominent philanthropist Bernard M. Baruch, this 16,000-acre property is dedicated to research and education. It includes numerous buildings and sites that reflect the lives of African Americans from the early 19th century through the first half of the 20th century. Among these are graveyards, extant villages, archaeological sites, rice fields, and roads. The most intact village is Friendfield which includes a "street" with five remaining structures. *Open Mon. through Fri., 9 a.m. to 3:30 p.m. and Sat., 9 a.m. to 2 p.m. Access or entry to the property is only by guided tour or programs.*

THE LOWCOUNTRY TRAIL AT BROOKGREEN GARDEN

1931 Brookgreen Garden Drive, Murrells Inlet

The Lowcountry Trail consists of a beautiful boardwalk that crosses the hillside overlooking Mainfield, a restored rice field of the former Brookgreen Plantation. For enslaved Africans at Brookgreen, this hill was a bridge between the world of daily work and life in the slave village beyond its crest.

Along the trail are interpretive panels that describe life on a rice plantation and four stainless steel figures that represent the "Plantation Owner," "the Overseer," an "Enslaved African Male," and an "Enslaved African Female." These figures serve as visually compelling landmarks to draw visitors along the trail and to interpret a revealing story about each one's role in the economic and social system of a Lowcountry plantation. *Open every day, 9:30 a.m. to 3:30 p.m.*

JAMES A. BOWLEY HOUSE

231 King Street, Georgetown

In the 1870s this was the home of James Alfred Bowley (circa 1844-1891). Born enslaved in Maryland, Bowley was the great nephew of Harriet Tubman. In 1850 Tubman and Bowley's free father organized a plan to free Bowley and his mother and sister, making them the first enslaved people whom Tubman helped emancipate. Bowley attended school in Philadelphia before rejoining his family in Canada. During the Civil War, he served as a landsman in the United States Navy. After the war, Bowley moved to Georgetown and worked for the Freedmen's Bureau as a teacher. By 1870 he had married Laura Clark (1854-1932) and lived at this location. They sold the home in 1880. Bowley served in the South Carolina House (1869-1874) and was a trustee for the University of South Carolina when it was briefly integrated after the Civil War. In 1874 a rivalry with another Black Republican led to a violent clash that made national news. Bowley also founded the short-lived *Georgetown Planet* newspaper.

MANSFIELD PLANTATION SLAVE STREET

1776 Mansfield Road, Georgetown

This rice-producing plantation was established in the 18th century. Records show that by 1860 there were over 100 enslaved people who planted 235 acres of rice at Mansfield. Six houses and a chapel remain. In 2004 descendants of slaveowner, F.S. Parker, opened a bed & breakfast inn on the site.

RICE MUSEUM
633 Front Steet, Georgetown

The historic Old Market Building and towering Town Clock are headquarters for the Rice Museum, which interprets the history of rice cultivation in Georgetown County. By 1750 Georgetown County was evolving as the center of the rice industry in the Carolina Colony, supported largely by the labor of enslaved West Africans. *Open Tues. through Sat., 12 p.m. to 4:30 p.m.*

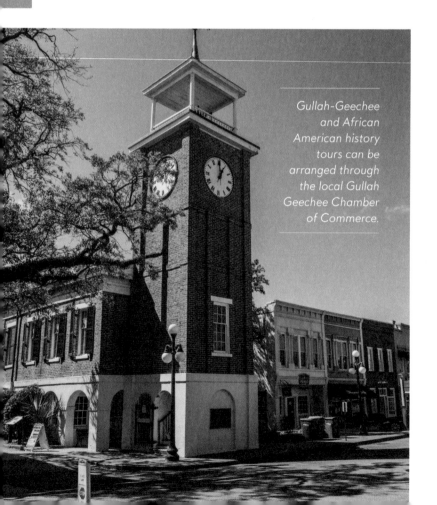

Gullah-Geechee and African American history tours can be arranged through the local Gullah Geechee Chamber of Commerce.

GULLAH MUSEUM

123 King Street, Unit 6, Georgetown

The Gullah Museum in Georgetown was founded by
community members Bunny and Andrew Rodriques. It uses Gullah
crafts and African artifacts to tell the story of the Gullah people
and the historic role they played in the building of South Carolina
and the United States. *Open by appointment only, the museum
offers presentations on topics ranging from Gullah Geechee history,
music, naming practices, food-to-crop cultivation, and animal
husbandry.*

FREEWOODS FARM

9515 Freewoods Road, Myrtle Beach

Freewoods Farm is the only African American living farm
museum in the United States. It recognizes and promotes the
contributions of African American farmers to the development of
agriculture in South Carolina and the nation. Situated on 40 acres
of land in the Burgess community of Myrtle Beach, Freewoods
offers hands-on education, documentation, and preservation of
the activities and practices of the small family farm structure that
defined the African American way of life after Emancipation. The
land is divided into three different educational experiences—
Freewoods Farm, Wetlands Preserve, and Main Street—displaying
unique components of the small farm community. As a non-profit,
Freewoods Farm welcomes volunteers who wish to experience how
previous generations lived their day-to-day lives. *Open Mon. through
Fri., 7 a.m. to 5 p.m and Sat., 2 p.m. to 5 p.m. Closed on Sunday.*

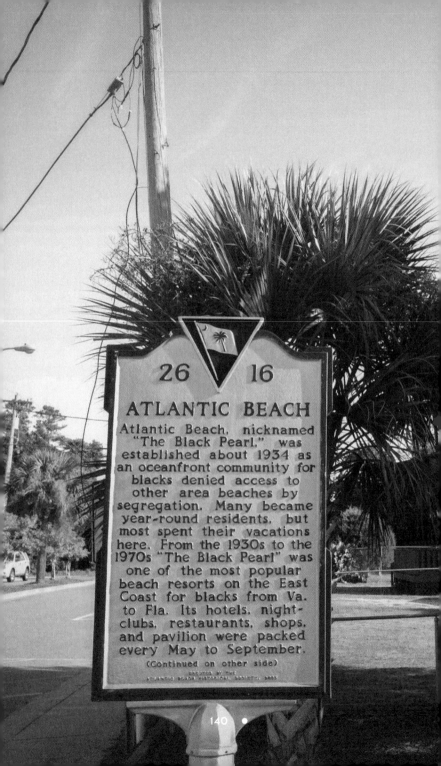

26 | 16

ATLANTIC BEACH

Atlantic Beach, nicknamed "The Black Pearl," was established about 1934 as an oceanfront community for blacks denied access to other area beaches by segregation. Many became year-round residents, but most spent their vacations here. From the 1930s to the 1970s "The Black Pearl" was one of the most popular beach resorts on the East Coast for blacks from Va. to Fla. Its hotels, night-clubs, restaurants, shops, and pavilion were packed every May to September.

(Continued on other side)

ERECTED BY THE
ATLANTIC BEACH HISTORICAL SOCIETY 2005

ATLANTIC BEACH

717 Atlantic Street

Atlantic Beach, nicknamed "The Black Pearl," was an oceanfront community for African Americans who were denied access to Myrtle Beach and other leisure sites due to segregation. Established around 1934, it soon became one of the most popular beach resorts along the Eastern Seaboard for Black travelers. Atlantic Beach hotels, nightclubs, restaurants, shops, and pavilion were popular destinations for locals and visitors of all ages. The beach saw fewer visitors after desegregation. Chartered in 1966, the town of Atlantic Beach is one of a few Black-owned oceanfront communities in the United States. A marker on site was erected by the Atlantic Beach Historical Society in 2005.

CHARLIE'S PLACE

1420 Carver Street, Myrtle Beach

Charlie and Sarah Fitzgerald opened Charlie's Place as a supper club in 1937. It was a stop on the "Chitlin' Circuit," nightclubs where Black entertainers such as Billie Holiday, the Mills Brothers, Little Richard, Ruth Brown, Otis Redding, and The Drifters performed during the era of racial segregation. While the club is gone, the Fitzgerald Motel, built in 1948, remains. The motel served Black entertainers who could not stay in whites-only hotels.

Oral tradition holds that "the Shag," a form of Southern swing dancing, originated here. Both white and Black customers gathered here to listen to music and dance. In 1950 the Ku Klux Klan led a parade through "The Hill," the African American neighborhood where Charlie's Place was located. The Klan returned later and shots were fired into the club, injuring many. Charlie was severely beaten but survived. Some Klansmen were charged, but no one was prosecuted.

HISTORIC MYRTLE BEACH COLORED SCHOOL AND EDUCATION CENTER

900 Dunbar Street, Myrtle Beach

The Myrtle Beach Colored School served African American students in the Myrtle Beach area for more than 20 years. Now, a Historic Myrtle Beach Colored School Museum and Education Center provides a window on that past, as well as a door to the future for all. Thanks to leadership from the City of Myrtle Beach, vision from former students, and a partnership among public and private entities, the old school has been preserved in spirit and recreated in fact and continues to fulfill an educational mission. *Open Mon., Weds., and Fri., 10 a.m. to 12 p.m.*

ST. MATTHEW BAPTIST CHURCH

1454 Tillman Road, Tillman

This church was founded in 1870 with Rev. Plenty Pinckney as its first minister and worshipped in a "bush tent" nearby until a log church was built a few years later. A new frame church was built on this site in the 1890s during the pastorate of Rev. C.L. Lawton. The present sanctuary was built in 1960 during the tenure of Rev. R.M. Youmans, who served here for more than 35 years. A marker was erected by the congregation in 2002.

THE GULF

Market Street between Liberty and Cheraw streets, Bennettsville

This area has been the center of the African American business district and a popular gathering place since the late 19th century. It has been called "the Gulf" since about 1925. Its most prominent early figure was E.J. Sawyer Jr. (1854-1929), who was born enslaved in North Carolina and came here about 1869. Sawyer was postmaster, principal of the Colored Graded School, and editor of the *Pee Dee Educator*. The area got its name from the large Gulf Oil Company sign at Everybody's Service Station. The street was often blocked off at night on the weekends for gatherings.

MARCH ON BALLOT BOXES

Tomlinson Street between Lexington Avenue & Eastland Avenue, Kingstree

On May 8, 1966, Dr. Martin Luther King Jr. visited Kingstree, where he urged an audience of 5,000 who had gathered on the grounds of Tomlinson High School to "march on ballot boxes" and use the vote as a means to pursue social and economic justice. King also called for grassroots mobilization and challenged each attendee to help register new voters. King referred to the moment as a "second Reconstruction" and reminded the audience that during the first Reconstruction, South Carolina had elected African American representatives to serve in the State House and US Congress, and could do it again.

AMAZING GRACE PARK /
CLEMENTA PINCKNEY MEMORIAL

307 W. Dozier Street, Marion

This city park was built in 2021 in honor of the late Senator Clementa Pinckney, who was killed along with eight other parishioners at Emanuel AME Church in Charleston in 2015. Pinckney spent his childhood summers in Marion and is buried nearby.

ABOUT THE PHOTOGRAPHER

Photographer, documentarian, and community organizer, Joshua Parks, is the Digital Programs and Community Engagement Specialist at the International African American Museum. Though Joshua was raised in Jacksonville, FL, his family history is deeply rooted in the Lowcountry, where he is a direct descendant of Sol Legare Island, a historic Gullah-Geechee sea island community. He is a graduate of Howard University and is completing his Masters degree in History at the College of Charleston. Trained as a public historian at the Avery Research Center for African American History and Culture, he specializes in social, political, and cultural histories of the African Diaspora.

Joshua has been a community organizer since 2015 and was instrumental in founding several local community-led projects and is involved in multiple national and international organizations that support mutual aid and community empowerment initiatives. He is a former secondary school educator who taught at both the middle and high school levels.

Some of Joshua's interests and hobbies include collecting vinyl records, film photography, and traveling.

ACKNOWLEDGMENTS

The WeGOJA Foundation and the South Carolina African American Heritage Commission gratefully acknowledge Dr. Barbara Williams Jenkins of Manning, SC, whose insistence on developing a hard copy Green Book kept it a priority within both organizations and led to its publication. As a career librarian and documentarian, Dr. Jenkins understood the timeless appeal of the physical record no matter the expedience and cost efficiency of its digital versions. She knew that online and internet records could not substitute for books, pamphlets, and journals any more than radio replaced newspapers, or television replaced radio.

A founding member of the SCAAHC, Dr. Jenkins served as chairwoman of the organization's Criteria Committee for more than a decade and helped identify African American historic sites that were under-represented in the state's archival and historical record.

This work was merely an extension of a lengthy career of chronicling and documenting history for public use. Much of it was devoted to working at South Carolina State University. Dr. Jenkins began as a librarian and served in many positions before retiring from the university as Dean and Professor of Library and Information Services.

With her keen interest in African American history, she was instrumental in the establishment of the South Carolina State College Historical Collection, where she and her staff oversaw and augmented special collections important to the university's history. Dr. Jenkins also helped to establish the South Carolina State College Historic District, which is full of historic markers for important structures and historical sites. She also worked with the

South Carolina Archives & History Commission to identify historic buildings and sites in Orangeburg and hosted preservation workshops to encourage others to preserve Orangeburg's significant African American history.

Dr. Jenkins is deeply involved in her community and Trinity AME Church and Williams Chapel AME Church. She is a member of the NAACP, The Links, Delta Sigma Theta Sorority Inc., and several historical and library boards of directors. She has been honored by the South Carolina Library Association, where she served as the first African American president; South Carolina State University; the American Library Association; and the South Carolina Black Hall of Fame. In 2019 she was given the state's highest civilian honor—the Order of the Palmetto

WeGOJA and SCAAHC also acknowledge Jannie Harriot of Hartsville, SC, another founding member of the Commission, who served in leadership roles for the organization for more than 25 years. Harriot was instrumental in collecting the funding and resources in 2017 to develop South Carolina's first African American online travel guide to historic places—GreenBookofSC. com—the precursor to this book.

Dawn Dawson-House
Executive Director
WeGOJA Foundation

Clementa Pinckney Memorial

INDEX BY COUNTY

UPSTATE

MIDLANDS

LOWCOUNTRY

THE GREEN BOOK IS BROUGHT TO YOU BY

Celebrating its 27th year in Spartanburg, **the Hub City Writers Project** serves readers and writers through its independent press, community bookshop, and diverse literary programming. Modeled after the Depression-era Federal Writers Project, Hub City seeks to foster a sense of community through the literary arts. Since its founding in 1995, Hub City has published more than 100 books and 800 authors and is particularly interested in books with a strong sense of place.

The mission of the South Carolina African American Heritage Commission is to identify and promote the preservation of historic sites, structures, buildings, and culture of the African American experience in South Carolina, and to assist and enhance the efforts of the South Carolina Department of Archives and History. **The WeGOJA Foundation** supports the efforts of the SCAAHC by developing resources to carry out its mission.

Set to open in Charleston in late 2022, the **International African American Museum** is a new museum of African-American history and culture that will **INTERNATIONAL AFRICAN AMERICAN MUSEUM** highlight the often overlooked history of African Americans in South Carolina and share how they helped shape North America and the world.

WITH THANKS TO OUR GENEROUS SPONSORS

ACKNOWLEDGMENTS

Hub City Press would like to thank the following people for their contributions to *The Green Book* project: Betsy Teter, Brad Steinecke, Brenda Lee Pryce, Dr. Glory Boozer, Nannie Jefferies, Cynthia Jeffers, Dr. Jim Neighbors, Richard Wheeler, and James Talley.

Thanks to Dawn Dawson-House and Joshua Parks who worked tirelessly on assembling the information and images in this book and were vital in envisioning the hard copy version of the Green Book mobile site that you are now holding.

Special thanks to our friends at the City of Spartanburg, in particular Assistant City Manager Mitch Kennedy. Thanks also to the Denny's Corporation for their help making this book a reality.

PHOTO CREDITS

Clementa Pinckney Memorial
City of Cheraw
DiscoverSouthCarolina.com
Equal Justice Initiative
Grand Strand Magazine / Will Williams
Historic Columbia
McMillan Pazdan Smith
One Columbia for Arts and Culture / Crush Rush
South Carolina State University
The Rice Museum
Spartanburg Public Library
Visit Rock Hill

PUBLISHING
New & Extraordinary
VOICES FROM THE
AMERICAN SOUTH

FOUNDED IN SPARTANBURG, South Carolina in 1995, Hub City Press has emerged as the South's premier independent literary press. Hub City is interested in books with a strong sense of place and is committed to finding and spotlighting extraordinary new and unsung writers from the American South. Our curated list champions diverse authors and books that don't fit into the commercial or academic publishing landscape.